Wilton Cookie Exchange

Dear Friend,

A plate filled with colorful homemade cookies is one of the most welcome sights of the holidays. The memories of your favorite holiday cookies may last, but the cookies disappear fast. You can never have enough on hand. That may be why so many people have rediscovered a wonderful holiday tradition—the cookie exchange. At a cookie exchange, you can share your favorite family recipes, find exciting new tastes and take home dozens of homemade cookies to serve your holiday guests. It's also a great celebration, the perfect way to kick off the season with friends and family.

Whether you're hosting or simply attending, Wilton Cookie Exchange will help you bring excitement and fun to the party. From creative invitations and table decorations to cookie designs unlike any others, this is the book you need to make the day merry.

As you can see on our cover, no one does holiday cookies like Wilton. Imagine arriving at the cookie exchange with treats like these! Our stand-up elves and gingerbread cabins, pearl-topped presents and sparkling trees are just a sample of the fun shapes you'll find inside Wilton Cookie Exchange. If you're looking for cookie inspiration, there's no better place than our Gallery section. Here, you'll see more than 150 easy and exciting decorating ideas in 6 favorite seasonal shapes—Snowflakes, Trees, Stars, Ornaments, Gingerbread Boys and Spritz. Use the Gallery to create a cookie sampler that will be the talk of the party, or choose your favorite designs and set up a decorating station that lets everyone join in the fun.

Holiday cookies should taste as great as they look. That's why we've collected some of our favorite recipes in Wilton Cookie Exchange. In addition to classics such as gingerbread and shortbread, you'll find tempting new tastes such as Butterscotch Chocolate Pecan Bars, Peppermint Ribbon Cookies and Almond Snowballs. Some of the best recipes were shared by Wilton employees in our Family Favorite Cookie Contest—they'll become favorites with your family as well.

If you are hosting, Wilton Cookie Exchange will help you coordinate every detail. Our Exchange Basics section is a blueprint for a successful event. It's filled with tips for creating fun, informative invitations, setting ground rules for guests, packaging cookies to look their most festive and more. There's even a week-by-week checklist for organizing your party without stress.

A cookie exchange can make the season brighter for everyone. Use Wilton Cookie Exchange as your guide to make it a holiday event you'll look forward to year after year.

Marvin Oakes
President
Wilton Enterprises

CREDITS

CREATIVE DIRECTOR
Daniel Masini

ART DIRECTOR/COOKIE DESIGNER
Steve Rocco

DECORATING ROOM SUPERVISOR
Cheryl Brown

SENIOR COOKIE DECORATORS
Mary Gavenda
Susan Matusiak

COOKIE DECORATORS
Jenny Jurewicz • Diane Knowlton
Mark Malak • Tracey Wurzinger
Michele Poto • Kathy Krupa
Kim Feledy • Michelle Boyd

RECIPE DEVELOPMENT
Nancy Siler • Gretchen Homan

EDITOR/WRITER
Jeff Shankman

WRITERS
Mary Enochs • Jane Mikis
Marita Seiler • Ann Wilson

PRODUCTION MANAGER
Challis Yeager

GRAPHIC DESIGN/PRODUCTION
Jill A. Blacketer

PHOTOGRAPHY
Peter Rossi - PDR Productions
Black Box Studios

FOOD STYLIST
Susie Skoog

PHOTO STYLIST
Carey Thornton

CREATIVE SERVICES ASSISTANT
Judi Graf

PRODUCT DEVELOPMENT/PUBLICATIONS
Tina Celeste

**WILTON FAMILY FAVORITE
COOKIE CONTEST WINNERS**
Doris Bohlig • Christina Dittmer
Lori Ellis • Sandy Folsom • Mary Gavenda
Carmella Markett • Sue Matusiak
Robin Mueller • Kathy Ryan • Julie Sobotta
Giulia Taraszkiewicz • Angela Thayer

COOKIE EXCHANGE MODELS
Denise Davis • Vicki Frasco
Lana Gardiner • Lisa Mullen
Joanne Winston • Tracey Wurzinger

IN U.S.A.
Wilton Industries, Inc.
2240 West 75th Street, Woodridge, IL 60517
www.wilton.com

RETAIL CUSTOMER ORDERS:
Phone: 800.794.5866 • Fax: 888.824.9520

CLASS LOCATIONS:
Phone: 800.942.8881
Online: www.wilton.com/classes/classlocator.cfm

IN CANADA
Wilton Industries Canada Company
98 Carrier Drive
Etobicoke, Ontario M9W5R1 Canada

RETAIL CUSTOMER ORDERS:
Phone: 416.679.0790

CLASS LOCATIONS:
Phone: 416.679.0790, ext. 200
E-mail: classprograms@wilton.ca

Contents

Enjoy the Give & Take!

cookie recipe

When all those beautiful cookies come together on the exchange table, everyone will be filled with the holiday spirit. On the pages to come, see how to create or contribute to the ultimate seasonal smorgasbord, with recipes, decorating ideas, presentation tips and more. No visions of sugar plums here—just the merriest homemade cookies you've ever seen!

Cookie Basics

Homemade cookies beat factory cookies every time. Only you can make holiday treats this festive-looking and fresh-tasting. The best thing—cookies aren't complicated. They just require a little common-sense care in order to reach their peak. Let's walk through the basics of mixing, baking and decorating. We'll share the easy steps you need to take to ensure quality cookies every time. Then, you'll be ready to share your expertise with your cookie exchange guests!

Essential Tools: Mixing

Using the right tools can help you avoid the main hazard of preparing cookie dough—overmixing. Start with a quality low-power hand mixer, then finish the job with a bowl scraper that provides good leverage for lifting the dense dough. The Wilton scrapers shown below all have comfort handles and blades shaped for superior leverage. Precise measurement is also essential for perfect consistency. The Wilton cups and spoons here feature an easy-to-read design and convenient pour spouts for perfect transfer to your mixing bowl.

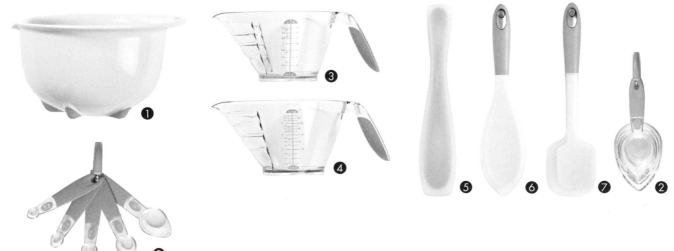

1. TILT-N-MIX BOWLS 2. SCOOP IT MEASURING SPOONS AND CUPS 3. 2 CUP LIQUID MEASURE
4. 4 CUP LIQUID MEASURE 5. SILICONE STAND MIXER SCRAPER 6. SILICONE SPOON SCRAPER
7. SILICONE UNIVERSAL SCRAPER

Essential Tools: Baking

An even-heating cookie sheet and quality cutters should be part of every baker's arsenal. Wilton has the largest selection of holiday shaped cutters along with anodized aluminum and non-stick cookie sheets for the best baking results. Other tools are equally important in preventing sticking of rolled dough and burned bottoms. Roll out dough with our non-stick pastry mat and rolling pin, sprinkled with a little flour. Line cookie sheets with Wilton Parchment for better baking and easy removal. For perfect portioning, use a one-squeeze cookie press like our Cookie Pro Ultra II or the Holiday Red Cookie Scoop.

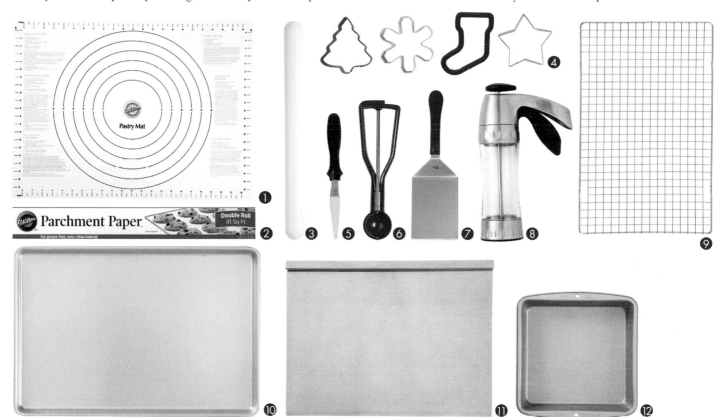

**1. PASTRY MAT 2. NON-STICK PARCHMENT PAPER 3. 20 IN. ROLLING PIN 4. ASSORTED WILTON HOLIDAY CUTTERS 5. SMALL TAPERED SPATULA
6. HOLIDAY RED COOKIE SCOOP 7. JUMBO COOKIE SPATULA 8. COOKIE PRO ULTRA II COOKIE PRESS 9. 10 X 16 IN. COOLING GRID
10. 12 X 18 X 1 IN. JELLY ROLL/COOKIE PAN 11. 14 X 20 IN. ALUMINUM COOKIE SHEET 12. 8 IN. SQUARE NON-STICK BISCUIT/BROWNIE PAN**

ABOUT BAKING PANS Sheets made of quality heavy-gauge aluminum provide the most even baking surface, without creating hot spots that can burn cookies. Some swear by non-stick sheets for easy release and cleanup; others prefer an uncoated surface prepared with non-stick cooking spray, shortening or parchment. While cookies may not spread as much on some non-stick pans, Wilton Non-Stick Cookie Sheets are designed to bake as well as our anodized sheets, with no adjustment for time or temperature needed. You may also choose an air-insulated sheet for added protection against burning. Cookie sheets should have very low sides or none at all. For bar cookies, use jelly roll, biscuit/brownie or sheet pans with sides about 1 to 2 in. high.

Essential Tools: Decorating

Keep Wilton toppings and tools on hand to create a great variety of cookie looks. Use Wilton bags and various tip shapes to create piped techniques. Or, ice smooth and top with colorful Wilton sugars, gels and nonpareils—no one has more colors and shapes for the holiday season.

**1. COLORED SUGAR 2. RAINBOW NONPAREILS 3. SPARKLING SUGAR 4. CINNAMON DROPS 5. SPATULA 6. FEATHERWEIGHT DECORATING BAG
7. MERINGUE POWDER FOR ROYAL ICING PREPARATION 8. SPARKLE GEL 9. ROUND, LEAF AND STAR DECORATING TIPS 10. READY-TO-USE COOKIE ICING**

How To Mix

For great cookie dough, remember 3 things: use quality ingredients, measure precisely and never overmix. Before you start, bring all ingredients to room temperature; cold eggs or liquids can change texture. Butter is best when slightly firm; using butter that is too soft can cause dough to spread.

OR

ELECTRIC MIXERS
Generally, you will want to use electric power to cream ingredients such as butter, sugar and eggs, then add flour and spices. Switch to hand power for the heavier dry ingredients. You may use an electric hand mixer with metal beaters or a stand mixer with paddle attachment; very stiff dough should not be mixed with a mixer, but rather by hand.

FINISHING BY HAND
Once the liquids are incorporated, gently mix in nuts or chips by hand, following recipe directions. For hand mixing, use a wide bladed, flexible scraper or spatula, preferably with a rounded bottom to get all ingredients incorporated.

Pre-Baking

Now that your dough is just right, it's important to handle it with care before it goes into the oven. That means rolling it out to a workable thickness, cutting precise shapes and getting it ready for baking on a properly-prepared cookie sheet. Some recipes may call for you to divide dough into disks and refrigerate before rolling. If so, remove each disk and let sit at room temperature for 10 minutes before you start.

Rolling Out Dough on Countertops

Rolling and handling dough too much can ruin the texture as much as overmixing. Your goal is to roll out dough evenly on a non-stick surface for easy release of cut shapes. Use a pastry mat to prevent sticking. A long non-stick rolling pin, lightly dusted with flour, will help you keep an even pressure while reducing the number of times you must re-roll.

1. Start with the rolling pin in the center of your dough disk. Roll with light, even pressure to the edge. Rolled dough should be about ⅛ in. thick; as a guide for consistent thickness, place a wooden dowel rod on either side of dough or use Rolling Pin Guide Rings.

2. Push cutter straight down to cut perfect shapes. Dip cutter into flour between cuts to prevent sticking.

3. Lift away dough around cut shapes and store for your next batch. Bake cookies following recipe directions.

Rolling Out Dough on Cookie Sheet

By rolling out dough directly on a prepared cookie sheet, you eliminate the step of transferring shapes and reduce the time dough sits before baking. Not having to move the cookies also lessens the risk that they will bend or tear on the way to the oven. With only one raised edge, a cookie sheet makes it easy to move your rolling pin evenly.

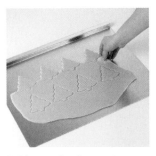

1. Place dough disk in center of pan. Roll from center of disk to each edge of pan using light, even pressure. Rolled dough should be about ⅛ in. thick; as a guide for consistent thickness, place an 11¾ in. lollipop stick on either side of dough or use Rolling Pin Guide Rings.

2. Push cutter straight down to cut perfect shapes, about 1 to 2 in. apart. Dip cutter into flour between cuts to prevent sticking.

3. Lift away dough around cut shapes and store for your next batch. Bake cookies following recipe directions.

Rolling & Baking on Parchment

Parchment is a happy medium for preparing and baking cookies. It's oven-safe, so you can use one sheet for rolling out, cutting and baking; you won't have to lift individual cookies onto your cookie sheet. With parchment, bottoms won't burn and clean-up is quick and easy; parchment is non-stick, so there's no need to use non-stick pan spray.

ROLL-OUT COOKIES
Many bakers like to roll out dough between 2 parchment sheets to prevent dough from sticking to the rolling pin. After rolling dough between parchment, lift off the top sheet and cut cookies. Remove dough around cut shapes, then bake cookies.

DROP COOKIES
A cookie scoop is a great tool for picking up consistent amounts of dough every time. Simply line your cookie sheet with parchment, scoop and drop the dough about 2 in. apart.

Working with Tinted Dough

Make any cookie merrier by adding color to the dough! Just a little icing color will make it easy to create festive cookies like the two-tone twists shown here. Tint dough a little darker than you would tint icing; cookies will bake lighter than dough appears. After dough is mixed, take out the portion to be tinted. Add just a little color with a toothpick. Gently blend color into dough using stand mixer paddle attachment, or knead in by hand. Stop to check the color. If it is too light, add a little more color and continue mixing until desired shade is reached.

1. For two-tone twists, roll logs of tinted and plain dough, about ½ in. diameter. Place side by side.

2. Starting at one end, twist logs together. Shape as needed to eliminate any gaps. Curve at the top to create a candy cane shape.

3. Bake and cool.

Piping with Thinned Dough

Unleash your cookie creativity! Tinted dough, thinned with water and piped with decorating bags and tips, lets you decorate cookies as colorfully as cakes or cupcakes. It's easy to achieve most basic techniques in any color you choose! Decorate with thinned dough before baking and the colorful design will bake right in.

1. Place desired portion of dough in small mixing bowl. Thin with 1 teaspoon water at a time until dough will pass through a tip. Place dough in decorating bag fitted with tip.

2. On cookie sheet, pipe outlines, dots, stars or zigzags to decorate your cookie.

3. Bake following recipe directions.

Adding Sprinkles & Sugars Before Baking

There's no faster way to spruce up holiday cookies! Top your cut shapes with sparkling sugar, nonpareils or jimmies for a quick color makeover, then bake. You can even use another cookie cutter as a guide for creating a festive shape on the cookie.

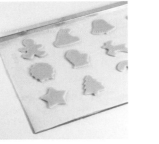

1. Position cut shapes 2 in. apart on cookie sheet.

2. Place a smaller or same-size cutter on the cookie. Pour Sprinkles or Sugars inside cutter.

3. Decorate cookies and bake according to recipe directions.

Pressing Spritz

Because cookie presses turn out so many cookies so fast, spritz are a great choice for a decorating station at your cookie exchange.

The secret to pressing with success is using room temperature dough which will pass easily through the cookie disk. Press directly onto your prepared cookie sheet. Don't worry if your first few spritz through the press aren't perfectly shaped; the dough will dispense more evenly as you go.

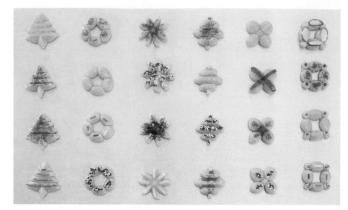

1. Shape dough into a log and place inside press. Hold press upright with the bottom ring resting firmly against a cooled ungreased cookie sheet (parchment paper not recommended). Squeeze the trigger to form a cookie.

2. Before baking, add fun toppings like cherries, almonds or nonpareils. After baking, pipe with icing, dip in candy or crushed peanuts.

Piped Meringue Cookies

Light and airy meringue cookies are the perfect alternative to heavy holiday treats. Because they are piped from a decorating bag onto the cookie sheet, you can create elegant shapes just as if you were piping icing. Try rosettes, swirls, stars or balls; you can add a festive touch of color by mixing colorful nonpareils into your recipe.

1. Fill decorating bag fitted with a large round or star tip like 1M or 4B with meringue. Follow techniques for piping desired design onto parchment-lined cookie sheet.

2. Add desired sprinkles. Follow recipe directions for baking. Let dry in oven, then transfer to cookie sheets to cool completely.

3. To keep meringues crisp, store in an airtight container. If cookies do soften, place in a 200°F oven to restore crisp texture.

Baking

Follow your recipe! It's the blueprint for baking success, with all the information you need about preheating the oven, preparing the pan, setting the temperature and baking time. With that said, for some recipes, you may want to adjust baking time to get the cookie texture you like. For crispier cookies, bake a little longer, for softer, chewier cookies bake less time.

USE A THERMOMETER Ovens can have a mind of their own, so a thermometer is your best tool to ensure when you should start baking. Check your cookies when you've reached the minimum baking time on the recipe, then continue baking if needed.

MOVE COOKIES TO COOLING GRID When baking's complete, let cookies rest on the sheet for a minute (unless otherwise directed). Use a spatula to lift cookies to a cooling grid and cool completely. Remember to cool your cookie sheet completely before placing the next batch of dough.

CUTTING BAR COOKIES For less crumbling and a clean look, score the cookies with a knife as soon as you take them from the oven. Cut only when completely cooled, following the score marks. Jelly and fruit fillings may stick to the knife, so wipe the blade frequently with a damp cloth.

Decorating Techniques

Why serve plain holiday cookies when it is so easy to add festive seasonal colors and fun toppings? Follow these easy decorating techniques for the merriest cookies to exchange, give or enjoy with your family.

Dipping

Perfect for parties. Just a simple dip in Light Cocoa Candy Melts and the fun begins!

1. Melt Candy Melts in microwave-safe bowl following package directions, or use the Wilton Chocolate Pro Electric Melting Pot. Dip cookie in candy.

2. Lift cookie, allowing excess candy to drip off.

3. Place on cookie sheet covered with parchment paper. Chill until firm.

Drizzling

Add artistic flair to cookies with just a drizzle of icing or melted candy. Drizzles don't have to be straight lines—try spirals, zigzags, and swirls, too.

1. Fill a parchment bag with melted candy or icing. Cut a small hole to create fine lines.

2. Drizzle cookie following pattern desired. Let set.

3. Try drizzling over the dipped area of cookies; let area set completely before drizzling.

Applying Sprinkles/ Sugars to Piped Icing

Your pretty icing accents will really stand out when you add a colorful treat topping. Be sure to add the sprinkles or sugar immediately after piping so they will stick.

1. Pipe desired design with royal or color flow icing.

2. Immediately sprinkle piped area with sugars or sparkles. Shake cookie to remove excess.

3. Let cookie completely dry before stacking or packaging.

Puddle Dots

Versatile disks of thinned royal or color flow icing are made in advance, dried, and used as accents, buttons and faces. Thin royal or color flow, adding ½ teaspoon water per ¼ cup icing. Icing is ready for flowing when a small amount dipped back into mixture takes a count of 10 to disappear. Add additional water as needed.

1. On waxed paper, pipe a ball, ¼ to 1¼ in. diameter depending on project instructions, using thinned icing in a cut parchment bag.

2. Let dry 48 hours.

3. Decorate following project instructions.

Color Flow

This icing creates a smooth, shiny look with color that really pops! It's sensational for seasonal cookies. The recipe is on p. 87.

1. Outline cookie using full-strength color flow icing and a round tip.

2. Thin icing and flow in using a cut parchment bag.

3. Let dry 8-12 hours.

Color Flow Dragging

Add detail and interest to decorated cookies while still maintaining the smooth, sophisticated look.

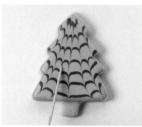

1. Outline and flow in icing following steps above. Immediately after flowing in, pipe lines of thinned color flow in a cut parchment bag.

2. Drag a toothpick through lines from end to end.

3. Let dry 8-12 hours.

Flow-In Designs

What a great look you can achieve when you flow in dots, swirls or other designs to wet color flow sections. The design dries into your iced top for a more exciting treat.

1. Outline and flow in icing following steps above.

2. Immediately after flowing in, pipe design using thinned color flow in a cut parchment bag.

3. Let dry 8-12 hours before further decorating.

Cookie Icing

Wilton Cookie Icing covers cookies with a shiny finish and dries quickly for easy stacking. It's great for decorating fun designs too. See the great holiday colors on p. 93.

1. Warm icing following bottle directions. Place cookie on cooling grid over drip pan. Squeeze icing over cookie to cover completely.

2. Tap grid gently to remove any bubbles and allow excess icing to drip off cookie.

3. Add sprinkles if desired while icing is still wet. Icing sets in about one hour.

Applying Sugars/ Sparkles after Baking

Adding toppings after baking may be preferred when using larger sprinkles or for filling in a design area with more control. During baking, jimmies or larger sprinkles may spread or colors may bleed.

1. Brush cooled cookie with piping gel.

2. Immediately add desired sprinkles or sugars.

3. Let set before packaging or stacking.

Tip Techniques

Stars

Stars are a natural for holiday decorating, whether filling in Santa's suit or topping off the tree. Great for borders too.

Icing: Royal (Medium Consistency) or Full-Strength Color Flow
Suggested Tips: 13, 16   **Bag Position:** 90° (straight up)
Hold Tip: Between ⅛ and ¼ in. above surface

  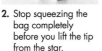

1. Hold bag in position with one hand while other hand holds the tip steady. Squeeze to form a star.

2. Stop squeezing the bag completely before you lift the tip from the star.

3. Lift the tip up and pull away from piped star.

Dots/Balls

Great for buttons, facial features and borders. The longer you hold in the tip as you pipe, the bigger the shape.

Icing: Royal (Medium Consistency) or Full-Strength Color Flow
Suggested Tips: 2, 3, 4, 5   **Bag Position:** 90° (straight up)
Hold Tip: Slightly Above Surface

1. Squeeze bag with even pressure. As icing builds up, raise tip, keeping end in icing.

2. Stop squeezing as you bring the end of the tip to the surface.

3. Lift tip up and pull away. Use edge of tip to shave any point so your shape is nicely rounded.

Leaves

Decorate wreaths, holly and vines with this easy pull-out technique.

Icing: Royal (medium consistency) or Full-Strength Color Flow
Suggested Tips: 349, 352   **Bag Position:** 45°
Hold Tip: Lightly Touching Surface; Wide Opening Parallel to Surface

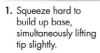 

1. Squeeze hard to build up base, simultaneously lifting tip slightly.

2. Relax pressure as you pull the tip toward you, drawing the leaf to a point.

3. Stop squeezing and lift away.

Outlining

Use simple lines to frame design areas, then pipe in with stars or zigzags. Great for hair and facial features, outlines are also essential for printed messages.

Icing: Royal (medium consistency) or Full-Strength Color Flow
Suggested Tips: 2, 3   **Bag Position:** 45°   **Hold Tip:** Slightly above surface

1. Touch tip to surface. Raise the tip slightly and continue to squeeze.

2. The icing will flow out of the tip while you direct it along the surface.

3. To end, stop squeezing, touch tip to surface and pull away.

Swirl Drop Flowers

The swirled look adds a nice motion effect. Squeeze and turn at the same time.

Icing: Royal (Medium Consistency) or Full-Strength Color Flow
Suggested Tips: 14, 225, 2 (for center)   **Bag Position:** 90° (straight up)
Hold Tip: For flower, lightly touching surface; for center, slightly above flower

1. Turn wrist in toward you before piping. Turn wrist a full twist, starting with the flat of your knuckles at 3:00 (9:00 for left-handers). As you

squeeze, slowly turn your hand, with knuckles ending at 12:00.

2. Stop squeezing and lift the tip away.

3. Make a dot flower center, keeping the tip buried as you squeeze. Stop squeezing, then pull tip up and away.

Shells

The basis for many borders as well as fleurs de lis. Lift the tip only slightly when piping shells to avoid a bumpy look.

Icing: Royal (Medium Consistency) or Full-Strength Color Flow
Suggested Tips: 13, 16   **Bag Position:** 45°   **Hold Tip:** Slightly above surface

1. Hold the bag in the 6:00 position in order to pull toward you.

2. Squeeze hard, letting icing fan out generously as it lifts the tip—do not lift

the bag. Gradually relax pressure as you lower the tip until it touches surface.

3. Stop pressure and pull tip away, without

lifting it off the surface, to draw it to a point. For a border, start next shell so that the fanned end covers the tail of the preceding shell to form an even chain.

Beads

This pretty border decoration uses a shell motion. To make a bead heart, pipe one bead, then a second, joining the tails. Smooth together using a decorator brush.

Icing: Royal (Medium Consistency) or Full-Strength Color Flow
Suggested Tips: 2, 3   **Bag Position:** 45°   **Hold Tip:** Slightly above surface

1. Squeeze as you lift tip slightly so that icing fans out.

2. Relax pressure as you draw the tip down and bring bead to a point.

3. For bead border, start next bead so that fanned end covers the tail of the preceding bead to form an even chain.

Zigzags

An easy up-and-down motion is all it takes to fill in outlined areas or pipe fur trim, pant cuffs and Santa's beard. Use a round tip to create tight, smooth zigzags or a star tip for a fuller, ridged look.

Icing: Royal (Medium Consistency) or Full-Strength Color Flow
Suggested Tips: Round–3, 5, Star–13, 16   **Bag Position:** 45°
Hold Tip: Lightly touching surface

1. Steadily squeeze and move hand in a tight up/down pattern.

2. Continue piping with steady pressure. To end, stop pressure and pull tip away. For elongated zigzags, move hand to desired height while keeping pressure steady. For a

more relaxed look, increase width as you move bag.

3. Repeat as you move in a straight line with consistent up/down motion.

Cookie Exchange Basics

Everything you need to know to stage a festive cookie celebration

If your cookie exchange is a hit, your guests will take home more than just wonderful cookies. With the right plan in place, they'll leave with many great memories, several new friends and the spirit of the season in their hearts. In this section, we'll help you plan it all, from sending the invitations and preparing a menu, to decking your walls and decorating your cookies for the holidays. Just as with your cookies, proper preparation and the right ingredients will help to make your celebration a holiday sensation!

Plan Ahead and Set the Tone

Remember that a cookie exchange is also a party. It requires the same preparation and planning as any holiday celebration—with fun foods, festive decorations and good company. The big difference is that for your cookie exchange to be a success, all your guests should go home with an equal amount of holiday cookies in many varieties. This calls for informative invitations, some clear ground rules for guests and the inevitable juggling of numbers when there are cancellations.

Set a Convenient Time and a Festive Theme

Pick a date in early December. Any later and invitees' calendars may be booked up. Call before sending invitations for a better idea of how many will attend. That way, you can give guests a number of cookies to bring.

Dream up a theme for the party in order to coordinate invitations, centerpieces and decorations. Survey the room to see where to set up the exchange table, a cookie-decorating station and refreshments.

Send Enticing, Informative Invitations

Merry invitations will get your guests as excited about attending the exchange as you are about hosting it! However festive you make them, it's even more important to use invitations to let guests know the rules that will make the exchange fun for all. Essential info includes:

PARTY PARTICULARS Date, time, place and a brief description of the event. Let guests know what they can expect for refreshments. There's nothing worse than preparing a meal only to discover that guests dined before they arrived. Announce that awards will be given too, with cookies judged on appearance, creativity and taste. A little friendly competition always makes the event more fun!

TALK ABOUT YOUR TREATS

Encourage your guests to share their recipes—and the stories behind them. Ask everyone to bring copies of recipes to stack next to its place card. Have each baker plan to talk about their cookies before you swap. Hearing about where the recipe originated, a helpful preparation tip or a favorite memory the cookies inspire makes the experience so much richer. As host, plan to record the revelry with a digital camera!

COOKIE EXCHANGE TIMELINE

Follow this checklist to keep you on track as you prepare for your cookie exchange.

FOUR WEEKS AHEAD
- ☑ Start a planning folder.
- ☐ Call friends to check on their availability.
- ☐ Finalize date and time.

THREE WEEKS AHEAD
- ☐ Dream up a theme.
- ☐ Buy or create invitations.
- ☐ Send invitations by mail or email.

TWO WEEKS AHEAD
- ☐ Prepare a menu.
- ☐ Survey your cabinets for serving and display pieces.
- ☐ Shop for holiday decorations, placecards, and tabletop embellishments.
- ☐ Bake cookies and purchase supplies for your decorating station.
- ☐ Purchase folders or albums for guests to take home all cookie recipes.
- ☐ Make award certificates.
- ☐ If necessary, bake and freeze batches of your cookies ahead of time. Defrost a day or two before the party, then add icing and decorations.

ONE WEEK AHEAD
- ☐ Double-check with invited guests to make sure they're planning on attending. If number of expected guests changes, adjust cookie count. Call guests to tell them they'll need to bring fewer or more cookies.
- ☐ Decorate your house.
- ☐ Finalize your menu.
- ☐ Shop for food and beverages.
- ☐ Create cookie-inspired decorations.
- ☐ Bake your cookies for the exchange. Store and wrap.

THE DAY BEFORE
- ☐ Make as many appetizers/entrees as possible and refrigerate.
- ☐ Set up tables for cookie exchange, buffet, cookie-decorating, and favors.
- ☐ Decorate tables and set out serving dishes and display stands.

THE DAY OF THE COOKIE EXCHANGE
- ☐ Finish foods and beverages for buffet.
- ☐ Set your cookies on the exchange table.
- ☐ Greet your guests and enjoy the day.

GUEST GROUND RULES Include a list of what guests should bring: number of cookies, containers for taking home, printed copies of recipes and a story or baking secret to share at the party. Typically, each guest should bring 12 cookies per person, including the host, and an extra dozen for snacking and judging.

To prevent disappointment, inform guests what treats are acceptable. Should only homemade treats be allowed or will bakery treats make the cut? Should baked goods be holiday-inspired or will classics like chocolate chip or oatmeal be welcome? To make the exchange more interesting, you may request cookies made from family recipes, those that represent a childhood memory or reflect ethnic heritage.

HELPFUL HINTS FOR COOKIES Include a list of cookie carrying ideas with invitations, encouraging pre-packing, to ensure safe transport to the party. Suggest presentation ideas (see page 18) as well as the following transportation tips:

1. Bake cookies 2 days before exchange.

2. Always cool before packing to prevent sticking.

3. Line cardboard containers with foil or plastic wrap to keep cookies fresh.

4. Place sheets of parchment between layers of cookies, especially those which are iced or decorated with royal icing*.

5. Pack delicate and decorated cookies in shallow containers; the fewer layers, the better.

6. Wrap cookies singly or in pairs and group wrapped cookies in a pretty box, bag or basket.

STACK SAFELY
Parchment sheets protect stacked cookies and are available in colorful holiday designs.

*Remember: Cookies iced with buttercream don't stack well.

Present your Cookies with Pride

Above: A winter-white box can still show off cookies colorfully. Use festive paper as accents; wrap bands to encircle the box, then embellish with textured ribbon and bow. Or, cut paper into favorite shapes like holly, ornaments, candy canes and trees to give your package instant season-right style.

Below: Look for colorful winter themed accents to brighten up your package. Here, a simple bow, artificial pinecone or poinsettia provide a fun finish. Or include the cookie recipe on the box. Make your own envelope by folding patterned cardstock into a pocket. Write the recipe on construction paper cut in a festive holiday shape.

Encourage guests to bring their amazing cookies in pretty packages. Prior to the party, clue your guests into the variety of merry materials available for wrapping cookies with ease, both on-line at www.wilton.com and www.eksuccess.com and in their home, including "found items" like colored plastic wrap or parchment and ribbon. When your exchange table starts to fill up with batches of festively-wrapped treats, it's like Santa's Workshop has come to your home.

Pretty presentation is also practical for your guests. It's a great way to speed up the swapping phase of the exchange. Pre-packaging also ensures that cookies retain their shape and taste. If guests mix different carry-home cookies in one large container, crisp cookies are likely to crumble, spicy gingerbread may overpower more delicately-flavored cookies and iced cookies may lose chunks of icing or decorations. Remember too that almost everyone will be giving cookies as gifts, so the exchange will be the perfect place to pick up wonderful wrapping ideas. As hostess, you can be the leader of the "pack". Here are some easy ways to dress up even plain Christmas cookies:

CAPTIVATING CONTAINERS Your choice of boxes and baskets is endless. You'll find a great selection of winter white boxes on page 95, ready to accent with your favorite colorful trims. Window boxes and popcorn-style cartons give a sneak-peek of the treats that await. You'll find a great selection of box shapes as well, from tent-style (perfect for biscotti) to rounds and hexagons!

Patterned plates and baskets are ready to be filled and wrapped in large treat bags for an impressive emporium-style presentation.

RICHLY-COLORED RIBBON For simple flair, ribbon can't be beat. It's that fast finishing touch that can help your box or basket stand out. Mix and match ribbon colors and textures to create more impact, as we've done in layered strips topped with a twist knot. Accessorize a patterned box with ribbon that picks up one of the colors; add strips strategically to frame a window or cut strips with patterned scissors to create more excitement. Visit www.eksuccess.com to see all the trims and tools at your disposal.

HOMEMADE COOKIE CONES

Guests will love to scoop up their cookies in these creative cones! With all the paper and ribbon styles available, it's easy to create a variety of looks. Cut a triangle from your favorite patterned card stock; finish the bottom edge with an elegant scalloped look using Cutter Bee scissors.

Curve the triangle into a cone and tape, then circle with wide ribbon, topped by a narrow bow and streamers. Add a fun handle by threading ribbon through small punched holes and secure with knots. Fill with cookies in a see-through bag.

SPIRITED STICKERS Want your cookie package to say "Happy Holidays"? A sticker can do just that! Merry messages, holiday colors and fun shapes like penguins and poinsettias—they're all part of what makes a sticker the fastest way to add personality to the presentation. You may be surprised at all the sticker styles available. Visit www.eksuccess.com for a great selection of dimensional stickers from Jolee's, which help you create a colorful layered accent to top off your treats.

Deck the Halls—and Your Table!

Cookie exchange decorations work best when they rise above the plated treats brought by guests. Clockwise from above: Let everyone grab a colorful shaped cookie ornament from your holiday tree. Create a village scene with cookie trees surrounded by stand-up house fronts. Build a winter centerpiece that doubles as a server, with cookie pops placed upright in a bowl filled with Sugar Pearls. Before the exchange, gather the family to build and decorate a traditional gingerbread house in a forest of sugar cone trees. Add a personal touch by placing a jolly gingerbread boy by every guest's cup.

Your baking buddies are much more likely to get in the spirit of the exchange if you set the scene with all kinds of dazzling decorations. Go all out! Tie in the theme of the celebration with your decor by using cookie-based accents, as shown here. Of course, your holiday tree, wreaths and poinsettias set a merry scene as well. In addition to festive sights, add satisfying sounds and scents. Create a playlist of jolly holiday music, light scented candles and have cider brewing on the stove.

Ideally, you will need to set up three different tables: one for serving refreshments, one for exchanging cookies and one for decorating cookies. Arrange the cookie-swap table so that all offerings can be seen and reached from at least two sides. Employ multi-tiered serving stands to keep various cookie designs in the spotlight and maximize tabletop space. Stands can also be dressed for the holidays with ribbon, sprigs of artificial evergreen and ornaments.

Enjoy The Day

Serve Fun Snacks

Don't knock yourself out cooking entrees and mixing beverages—after all, this is a day devoted to sharing cookies and camaraderie. Opt for simple spreads, such as coffee and cake or cocktails and canapés, or pull together an easily assembled buffet. Whether you're serving brunch, lunch, afternoon tea or dinner, keep the bill of fare on the light and savory side. Save the cookies for judging and trading.

Take your cooking cue from cookie shapes and cookie-making methods to fashion original, edible works of art. Utilize Christmas-motif cookie cutters to shape fancifully formed open-face sandwiches—top with piped-on spreads in holiday hues. Create spritz-like cheese pastries using a cookie press. Use snowman or Christmas tree cake pans to mold gelatin salads or seafood mousses.

Supply a holiday-themed dessert that can double as a centerpiece. Wilton has a great selection of holiday pans for creating cakes, molded salads and desserts in favorite seasonal shapes. You can even display a mega-sized decorated cookie to serve everyone—press chocolate chip, sugar or shortbread dough into one of our shaped pans, bake and cool, then decorate to complement the shape.

LET GUESTS BE CREATIVE

Decorating cookies at the exchange can really bring the crowd together. Set up a decorating station with plain cookies and all the icing, tools and trims needed to transform them. You'll need bags, tips and spatulas, tube icings and gels, edible color markers and plenty of sprinkles and sugars. Keep this book on hand for inspiration!

Host a Friendly Competition

Make every guest feel like a winner. Hold an award ceremony for best baked goods. Have each guest bring extra cookies to share with a jury of their cookie-baking peers. Distribute ballots to guests after tasting is complete. Prizes could be ribbons, computer-generated certificates, or trophy-like cookies on a stick. Be prepared to present as many awards as there are guests. Categories could include: Best-Dressed Cookie; Best Chrismas Character; Best Use of Chocolate; Best Overall Presentation; Best Sprinkles in a Supporting Role; Best Ethnic Recipe; Best Icing Design; Best Shortcake Production; Best Buttery Taste; Best Color Combination; and Most Festively Iced.

Say Thanks for Sharing

Present guests with a cookie-making memento that's fun and functional. Place cheerfully wrapped or ribboned favors on a small table set near the front door so guests will remember to tote them home. Make the giveaway display extra jolly by trimming a tabletop tree with ribbon suspended cookie cutters, measuring spoon sets, and colorful spatulas. Or, fill small gift bags with a pack of Christmas Cookie Stencils, a FoodWriter Edible Colored Marker, and Colored Sugars. No matter the presentation, a cookie-themed gift guests can take home with their treats will always remind them of the wonderful time they shared at your cookie exchange.

COOKIE GALLERY

Variety is the spice of life and a sure way to be popular at the cookie exchange! Our Cookie Gallery will show you all the great designs you can create from a few basic cookie shapes. After your cookies have cooled, gather all your tools and trims in one place and have fun decorating a sensational holiday sampler to take to the party. Or, use our gallery ideas if you're planning a decorating station at the exchange. Give every guest a task—spreading icing, piping candy or adding toppings. It's a great way to break the ice and share the holiday spirit!

For specific technique instructions, see pages 11 - 13.

SPRITZ

Our easy-to-use cookie press (p. 88), loaded with Classic Spritz Cookie Dough (p. 86), is the perfect tool for making many festive cookie shapes fast— just what you need for your cookie exchange! Here are over 3 dozen great ways to decorate!

Fun Flecks
Pipe lines of melted Red Candy Melts. Sprinkle with White Nonpareils.

Pecan Petals
Pipe edge and center designs with melted Light Cocoa Candy Melts; sprinkle with ground pecans.

Our Family Tree
Press cookie with green tinted dough. Pipe lines with melted White Candy Melts; add Snowflake Mix Sprinkle and Christmas Nonpareils.

Dipped Delight
Dip in melted Light Cocoa Candy Melts; sprinkle with ground pecans.

Blossoming Brightly
Outline petals with melted Red Candy Melts; sprinkle with Red Colored Sugar and top with Christmas Confetti Sprinkle.

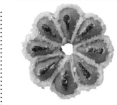

Festive Wreath
Press cookie with green-tinted dough. Pipe petals and centers with melted Red and White Candy Melts. Sprinkle with White Sparkling Sugar.

Snowy Spruce
Press cookie with green-tinted dough. Pipe lines of melted White Candy Melts. Attach Sugar Pearls and Jumbo Snowflake Sprinkle.

Holiday Hybrid
Drizzle with lines of melted Red and White Candy Melts. Sprinkle with Colored Sugars and attach Sugar Pearls.

Ruby Rings
Pipe circles and dots with melted Red and Green Candy Melts. Sprinkle circles with Red Colored Sugar.

Rainbow Garlands
Press cookie with green-tinted dough. Pipe lines and dot with melted White Candy Melts; attach 6-Mix Jimmies and Snowflake Mix Sprinkle.

Winter Intersection
Pipe circles with melted White Candy Melts. Sprinkle with Christmas Nonpareils.

Open Flower
Outline cookie and add outline and dot details with Red Candy Melts. Sprinkle with Red Colored Sugar and attach Green Jimmies from 6-Mix Assortment with White Candy Melts.

Snow Bloom
Press cookie with green-tinted dough. Outline petals with melted White and Red Candy Melts. Attach Jumbo Snowflake Sprinkle at center.

Diagonal Drizzle
Drizzle with diagonal lines of melted Green and Red Candy Melts.

Holiday Boutonierre

Outline cookie and add detail with lines of melted White Candy Melts. Sprinkle with Red and Green Colored Sugar and attach Jumbo Snowflake Sprinkle at center.

Christmas Pick

Decorate petals with zigzags in melted Blue Candy Melts; pipe dot center in melted Light Cocoa Candy Melts.

Arctic Arbor

Press cookie using green-tinted dough. Drizzle with lines of melted Red and White Candy Melts. Sprinkle with Christmas Nonpareils.

Awesome Ornament

Pipe dots and outlines with melted Red Candy Melts. Cover dots with Red Colored Sugar; attach Christmas Confetti on outlines.

Floral Flip

Pipe spirals with melted Light Cocoa Candy Melts; attach Cinnamon Drop center.

Nutty & Nice

Outline cookie with melted White Candy Melts; sprinkle with Christmas Nonpareils. Attach slivered almonds with melted candy.

Frosty Flower

Outline sections with melted Blue Candy Melts. Sprinkle with White Sparkling Sugar.

One Golden Ring

Outline cookie and dot tops with melted White Candy Melts; sprinkle sides with White Nonpareils and top with Gold Pearlized Sugar.

Sunburst Center

Outline cookie and divisions with melted White Candy Melts. Sprinkle with Red and Green Pearlized Sugar.

Colors Comingle

Pipe in sections with melted White Candy Melts; sprinkle with Rainbow Nonpareils. Attach Christmas Confetti at center with melted White Candy Melts.

Holiday Hues

Pipe in sections with melted White Candy Melts; sprinkle with Christmas Nonpareils. Attach Christmas Confetti at center with melted candy.

Tree Jewelry

Drizzle with lines of melted Red Candy Melts. Pipe a dot of melted White Candy Melts at top and bottom; attach Christmas Confetti.

Swirls & Pearls

Pipe spirals with melted Red Candy Melts. Attach Sugar Pearls at center.

Yule Yellow

Pipe circles of melted Yellow Candy Melts. Sprinkle with Yellow Colored Sugar.

Snow Crunch Ornament

Pipe in sections with melted White Candy Melts; sprinkle with White Nonpareils. Attach Christmas Confetti with dots of melted candy.

Purple Posy

Pipe in sections with melted White Candy Melts; sprinkle with Violet Colored Sugar. Attach Christmas Confetti center with melted candy.

Wreath Splendor

Press cookie using green-tinted dough. Attach Cinnamon Drops with melted Green Candy.

Trimmed Tree

Press cookie using green-tinted dough. Pipe trim with piping gel. Sprinkle with Yellow Colored Sugar. Attach Jumbo Star Sprinkle with melted candy.

Splashy Scarlet

Pipe in sections with melted Red Candy Melts; sprinkle with Red Colored Sugar.

Greenery

Pipe spirals with melted Green Candy Melts. Attach Cinnamon Drop center.

Tree Trinket

Drizzle cookie with lines of melted Red and White Candy Melts. Sprinkle with Green Pearlized Sugar.

Go Green!

Outline cookie with melted White Candy Melts; sprinkle with Green Pearlized Sugar. Attach Jumbo Snowflake Sprinkle at center with melted candy.

Red to Remember

Outline cookie with melted White Candy Melts; sprinkle with Ruby Pearlized Sugar. Attach Sugar Pearl at center.

Blue & White Blast

Pipe in sections with melted White Candy Melts; sprinkle with White Nonpareils. Attach Jumbo Snowflake Sprinkle at center.

Raise the Bar

Dip cookie in melted White Candy Melts. Drizzle lines of melted Green Candy Melts; sprinkle with Christmas Nonpareils.

GINGERBREAD PEOPLE

Attract a crowd at the cookie exchange with your jolly gingerbread people! With all our fun ways to dress them up, there's no easier cookie to personalize for the holidays. Start with the classic Gingerbread recipe (p. 86) and our 3 Pc. Gingerbread Cutter Set (p. 89), then follow the easy decorating instructions here, using royal icing (unless otherwise specified) and dazzling Sprinkles.

Wrapped up for Winter
Pipe dot and outline facial features, ear muffs and buttons. Pipe in scarf and shoes.

Fast Friend
Pipe dot and outline facial features, zigzag cuffs and swirl hair.

Buttoned Up
Outline cookie; add dot and outline facial features. Attach spice drop halves for buttons.

Granny's in her Glory
Outline and pipe in top; pipe ruffle skirt. Add swirl hair, dot eyes and nose, outline mouth and bead trim. Attach Christmas Confetti at waist.

Jolly Jumper
Ice overalls and hat smooth; sprinkle with Red and Green Colored Sugar. Pipe shirt, facial features, buttons and swirl hat trim.

Short Winter
Outline and pipe in shorts and suspenders; add dot and outline details. Attach Flowerful Medley confetti on eyes, cheeks and clothes.

Christmas in Crimson
Ice clothes smooth; sprinkle with Red Colored Sugar. Pipe dot and outline facial features, scallop and zigzag cuffs. Add swirl hair and dot buttons.

Shiny and Bright!
Cover with thinned color flow. Immediately pipe in details.

Holiday Baker
Ice dress and shoes smooth; let dry. Ice apron smooth. Pipe dot, outline and zigzag facial features and details.

Dressed for Chill
Pipe dot and outline facial features. Attach Christmas Confetti scarf and cuffs.

The Wild Vest!
Outline and pipe in vest. Pipe pull-out hair, dot and pipe-in facial features. Add dot and outline vest details.

Greetings in Green
Outline and pipe in shirt and dress. Pipe outline mouth and hair, dot and swirl facial features, buttons and dress trim.

Bowtie Guy
Pipe outline and dot clothes and facial features.

Berry Christmas!
Ice clothes smooth. Pipe outline hair, pipe-in bow, dot knot, eyes and nose. Pipe scroll and zigzag trim, dot berries and leaves.

Striking Stripes
Ice skirt smooth. Outline shirt and pipe stripes. Add swirl hair, dot and outline facial features and skirt trim.

Cute as a Button
Outline cookie and fill in with stars. Add dot and outline facial features; attach Flowerful Medley confetti.

A Nonpareil Noël
Pipe dot buttons, zigzag cuffs, outline and pipe-in bowtie; sprinkle with Colored Sugar or Nonpareils. Add dot and outline facial features.

Sporting Shorts
Ice shorts smooth; pipe in suspenders and bow tie; sprinkle with Colored Sugar or Nonpareils. Pipe dot eyes and nose, outline hair and mouth.

Peppermint Print
Ice clothes smooth. Pipe outline stripes, hair, bows and mouth. Pipe dot eyes, nose and cheeks. Attach Christmas Confetti at hem.

Snowflake Smock
Pipe swirl hair. Outline dress; pipe dot and outline facial features and dress details, zigzag hem and scallop sleeves.

A Child Smiles
Cover with thinned color flow; let dry. Outline and flow in shorts. Pipe dot and outline details; attach Christmas Confetti cuffs.

Simply Merry!
Outline body with zigzags. Pipe dot eyes, nose and buttons, outline mouth.

Holiday Spice
Pipe outline hair and mouth, dot eyes and nose. Roll out spice drops on waxed paper sprinkled with sugar. Cut clothes and bow; attach with dots of icing.

TREES

Choosing the best-looking Christmas tree is always difficult. The good news is that you can choose all these tree cookies for your cookie exchange assortment. Your fellow partygoers will have the tough decision—with so many fun shapes and cool colors, they won't know which to take home! Use our 3 Piece Christmas Trees Cutter Set, (p. 89) royal icing (unless otherwise noted) and bright sprinkles and sugars to grow your festive forest.

Two-tone Tree
Roll together diagonal strips of light and dark green-tinted dough; cut and bake cookies.

Flocked Fir
Outline and flow in with color flow, let dry. Pipe zigzag section lines and coat with White Sparkling Sugar.

Rainbow Glow
Ice star smooth and pipe in trunk. Cover tree with pull-out leaves; sprinkle with Rainbow Nonpareils.

Alpine Shine
Use green-tinted dough. Brush cookie with piping gel after baking; sprinkle with Rainbow Nonpareils.

Blended Branches
Outline and flow in with light green color flow. Immediately flow in darker green color flow; drag out branch lines with toothpick.

Sparkling Sapling
Brush cookie with piping gel; sprinkle with White and Green Sparkling Sugar. Ice trunk smooth.

Zesty Zigzags
Use green-tinted dough. Pipe outline star points and zigzag branches.

Textured Tree
Cover tree and trunk with zigzags; overpipe branch divisions with smaller zigzags. Pipe dot lights.

Scallops & Star
Use green-tinted dough mixed with a little yellow. Ice star area smooth and sprinkle with Yellow Colored Sugar. Pipe scallops and coat with Light Green Colored Sugar.

Winter Glitter
Use green-tinted dough. Ice tree smooth; pipe outline branches. Sprinkle with Dark Green Colored Sugar and zigzag stem.

Snow-Tipped Tree
Use green-tinted dough. Ice star smooth; pipe zigzag branches and pull-out snow.

Winter White Tree
Outline and flow in with color flow. Immediately attach Sugar Pearls; let dry. Brush with White Pearl Dust.

Colorbright Conifer
Use green-tinted dough. Pipe lines of red and green across tree; sprinkle with matching Colored Sugars.

Showered with Snow
Use green-tinted dough. Pipe tip 1 outline and dot snowflakes.

Softly Scrolled
Use green-tinted dough. Pipe outline scrolls and dots.

Electric Evergreen
Outline and flow in with color flow, let dry. Pipe outlines and dots in graduated sizes.

Dazzling Drifts
Outline cookie with full-strength color flow. Flow in zigzag sections of thinned color flow.

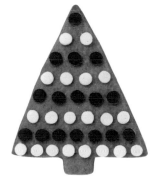

Ornament Excitement
Use green-tinted dough. Attach Christmas Confetti with dots of icing.

Neon Noël
Outline cookie; fill in with stars. Pipe in stem. Attach Flowerful Medley confetti with dots of icing.

Pearl Pine
Outline cookie with full-strength color flow; flow in with thinned color flow. Immediately attach Sugar Pearls.

Aspen You Shall Receive
Outline cookie with full-strength color flow; flow in with thinned color flow. Let dry. Pipe pull-out branches; sprinkle with White Cake Sparkles.

Grand Garland
Use green-tinted dough. Pipe zigzag garlands and dots.

Fluffy Fir Tree
Decorate branches and trunk with zigzags, decorate star with dots.

SNOWFLAKES

No two snowflakes are exactly alike, which makes these festive flakes perfect for your cookie exchange or holiday gift sampler! With our great selection of cutters, icings and sprinkles, starting on p. 88, it's easy to give each cookie its own cool colors and fun shape. Decorate with color flow icing unless otherwise noted.

Snowy Swirls
Outline and flow in cookie; let dry. Pipe swirls.

Gentle Snowfall
Outline and flow in cookie; let dry. Pipe outline starbursts and dots.

Polar Pearls
Outline and flow in cookie; let dry. Add teardrop loops and dot accents; let dry. Brush with White Pearl Dust.

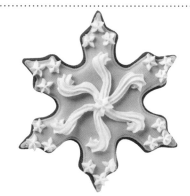

Star Shower
Outline and flow in cookie; let dry. Pipe reverse shell pinwheel center and star detail.

Chocolate Cool
Make chocolate orange roll-out cookies. Decorate with royal icing loops, fleurs de lis and dots.

Violet Vibrance
Use melted White Candy Melts (tinted violet using Garden Candy Color Set); pipe outline veins. Sprinkle veins with Lavender Colored Sugar.

Winter White
Outline and flow in cookie, let dry. Pipe swirl details and dot center.

Icy Blue
Outline and flow in cookie; let dry. Pipe outline veins; sprinkle with Blue Pearlized Sugar.

Scarlet Shells
Pipe royal icing shells and reverse shells; decorate with Sugar Pearls.

Gold Flake
Outline and flow in cookie; let dry. Pipe outline veins and dot center; brush with Gold Pearl Dust/lemon extract mixture.

Silver Scrolls
Outline and flow in, let dry. Add swirls and dot center. Brush design with Silver Pearl Dust/lemon extract mixture.

Golden Garden

Outline and flow in cookie, let dry; top with swirl drop flowers with dot centers. Brush flowers with Gold Pearl Dust/lemon extract mixture.

Fudgy Flurries

Make chocolate orange roll-out cookies. Decorate with royal icing dots.

Fancy Flake

Make chocolate orange roll-out cookies. Decorate with royal icing fleurs de lis and puddle dot center brushed with White Pearl Dust.

Well-Placed Pearls

Outline and flow in cookie; let dry. Pipe outline veins and attach Sugar Pearl accents.

Bold Blizzard

Outline and flow in cookie. Immediately pipe in red outline veins; let dry. Decorate with puddle dot center.

Pearlescent

Outline and flow in cookie; let dry. Pipe outline veins; top with puddle dots brushed with White Pearl Dust.

Aqua Sparkle

Outline and flow in cookie. Let set 3 to 5 minutes then sprinkle with white Sparkling Sugar.

Flakes with Flair

Outline cookie with red and flow in with green; let dry. Pipe outlines and reverse shell-motion detail, add dots.

Snow Dancing

Make chocolate orange roll-out cookies. Attach Jumbo Snowflake Sprinkles with dots of royal icing.

Green Sheen

Outline and flow in cookie; let dry. Pipe outline veins; sprinkle with Emerald Green Pearlized Sugar.

Graceful Lace

Outline and flow in cookie; let dry. Pipe cornelli lace.

Heart of Winter

Outline and flow in cookie; let dry. Pipe outline and fill-in hearts in white topped by dot and scroll detail; let dry. Brush hearts with White Pearl Dust.

STARS

Cookies that deserve star billing at your exchange table! It's amazing that with just our Comfort Grip Star Cutter (p. 89), you can make a galaxy of eye-popping designs. Using great effects like Pearl Dust, pulled color flow and Sparkling Sugar, your stars will dazzle everyone! Decorate with royal icing unless otherwise noted.

Cocoa Corona
Cover baked cookie with melted Light Cocoa Candy Melts. Pipe swirls, then brush with Gold Pearl Dust/lemon extract mixture.

Cool Blue
Outline and flow in with color flow; let dry. Pipe outline snowflake veins; sprinkle with White Sparkling Sugar.

Earn a Gold Star
Ice cookie smooth in yellow. Mark inner star with smallest cutter from Nesting Star Set. Outline and pipe in inner star and edge cookie in white; sprinkle with White Nonpareils.

Sprinkled with Stardust
Before baking, cover cookie with Red Pearlized Sugar.

Spun Silver
Outline and flow in with color flow; let dry. Drizzle lines of color flow; let dry, then brush with Silver Pearl Dust/lemon extract mixture.

Star Spotted
In advance, pipe puddle dots from ⅛ to ⅝ in.; let dry, then brush with Gold Pearl Dust/lemon extract mixture. Outline and flow in cookie with color flow; let dry, attach dots with icing.

Dashing Dots
Ice cookie smooth; position Jumbo Rainbow Nonpareils.

Golden Sunshine
In advance, pipe ½ in. puddle dot center; let dry, then brush with Gold Pearl Dust/lemon extract mixture. Outline and flow in cookie with color flow; let dry. Pipe lines; brush with Pearl Dust mixture; attach puddle dot.

Cinnamon Star
Ice cookie smooth. Attach Cinnamon Drops on edge.

Spiral Sparkle
Outline and flow in with color flow; let dry. Pipe swirls and brush with Gold Pearl Dust/lemon extract mixture.

Pinpoint Panache
Before baking, sprinkle cookie with Christmas Nonpareils.

Holly Sprig Star
Outline and flow in with color flow; let dry. Outline and pipe in holly; pipe dot berries.

Swirled Supernova
Ice cookie smooth. Pipe outlines and swirls.

Twin Stars
Mark inner star using smallest Nesting Star Cutter. Fill in marked area with stars.

Drizzle Dazzle
Cover cookie with melted Light Cocoa Candy Melts and drizzle lines of melted Red and Green Candy Melts.

Stained Glass Star
Outline cookie and star sections; brush lines with Gold Pearl Dust/lemon extract mixture. Fill in with stars.

Candy Cane Comet
Pipe stripes of red and white, sprinkling each with matching Red Sugar and White Sparkling Sugar as you decorate.

Wild Whirl
Drizzle cookie with thinned color flow.

Dots Connect!
Before baking, position Christmas Confetti on cookie.

All-Star Sensation
Brush baked cookie with Piping Gel and position Green Nonpareils on cookie.

Energy Waves
Outline and flow in with white color flow. Immediately flow in inner star outlines of red and green; drag out designs with toothpick.

Twinkle Sprinkle Little Star
Before baking, cover cookie with Red and White Sparkling Sugar.

In Orbit!
In advance, make a ½ in. puddle dot; let dry, then brush with White Pearl Dust/lemon extract mixture. Outline and flow in cookie with color flow; let dry. Pipe starburst lines and sprinkle with Blue Sugar; attach Sugar Pearls and puddle dot.

ORNAMENTS

Here are the cookies your exchange guests will be hanging around! Just like the family tree-trimming event, everyone will want to grab ornaments featuring their favorite colors and holiday designs. Cut cookies using the medium round cutter from our 101 Cookie Cutter Set (p. 90), or the fancy ornament from our 3 Pc. Holiday Cutter Set (p. 89). Decorate with royal icing unless otherwise noted.

Color Wave

Outline sections and flow in with color flow; let dry. Pipe in hanger. Brush outlines and hanger with Gold Pearl Dust/lemon extract mixture.

Mad about Plaid

Outline and flow in with color flow. Pipe outlines, stars and zigzag hanger. Brush stars and hanger with Gold Pearl Dust/lemon extract mixture.

Striped Sizzle

Pipe stripes of red, light and dark green, sprinkle each with matching Colored Sugar as you decorate. Pipe zigzag hanger.

Merry Message

Outline and flow in with color flow; let dry. Pipe curvy vine with pull-out leaves. Pipe dot berries, let dry; print message and pipe zigzag hanger.

Bright Brocade

Outline and flow in with color flow; let dry. Edge center stripe area with beads, swirls and dots and pipe zigzag hanger. Brush accents with Gold Pearl Dust/lemon extract mixture.

Vibrant Violet

Outline and flow in sections with color flow; let dry. Pipe spirals, dots, outlines and beads; brush with Silver Pearl Dust/lemon extract mixture. Pipe in sections with Piping Gel; sprinkle with Blue Colored Sugar.

Polka Dot Punch

Ice cookie smooth. Attach Christmas Confetti and mini marshmallow half for hanger.

Try a Tree!

Outline and flow in with color flow; let dry. Pipe outlines on sections and pull out branches of tree. Add dots. Pipe circle around tree; sprinkle with White Sparkling Sugar.

Fun Flake

Outline and flow in cookie with color flow; let dry. Outline snowflake; add dot accents (flatten and smooth with finger dipped in cornstarch). Pipe zigzag hanger.

Peppermint Pinwheel

Outline and flow in sections with color flow; let dry. Pipe zigzag hanger.

Dot Drop

Outline and flow in cookie with color flow; let dry. Pipe section lines and zigzag hanger; sprinkle lines with White Nonpareils. Pipe dots.

Chevron Chic
Outline and flow in sections with color flow; let dry. Pipe outlines, beads and chevron designs; brush chevrons with piping gel and coat with Green Colored Sugar.

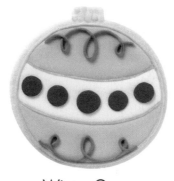

Winter Green
Outline and flow in sections with color flow; let dry. Pipe dots at center (pat smooth with finger dipped in cornstarch). Pipe loops on ends and zigzag hanger.

Glittering Gem
Outline and pipe in sections in red and white; sprinkle each section with matching Red Sugar and White Sparkling Sugar. Pipe zigzag hanger.

Ice Flow
Outline and flow in cookie with color flow; let dry. Pipe in icicle area and coat with White Cake Sparkles. Attach mini marshmallow half for hanger.

The Word Most Heard
Outline and flow in cookie with color flow; let dry. Pipe outline letters and zigzag hanger; brush hanger with Silver Pearl Dust/lemon extract mixture.

Holly's Hanging
Outline and flow in sections with color flow; let dry. Pipe leaves and dot berries. Decorate ends with outlines, scallops and beads in red piping gel; sprinkle with Red Colored Sugar.

Emerald Excitement
Outline and flow in cookie with color flow; let dry. Pipe zigzag hanger, outlines, x's and dots; brush with Gold Pearl Dust/lemon extract mixture. Attach Sugar Pearls at center of each x.

Joyful Boy
Outline and flow in cookie with white color flow; let dry. Stencil brown gingerbread boy design from Cupcake and Cookie Stencils Set. Pipe scallop border and dots, add zigzag hanger.

Golden Grandeur
Outline and flow in cookie with color flow; let dry. Pipe zigzag hanger, scrolls, outlines and dots; brush accents with Gold Pearl Dust/lemon extract mixture.

Season's Greeting
Outline and flow in sections with color flow; let dry. Pipe outlines and fill in accents; sprinkle with Red Colored Sugar. Print message.

Stylized Snowflake
Outline and flow in cookie with color flow; immediately flow in branches of snowflake. Let dry. Pipe outline veins and dot accents. Attach mini marshmallow half for hanger.

Bright White
Ice cookie smooth. Pipe zigzags and sprinkle with matching Colored Sugar. Pipe dots. Attach mini marshmallow half for hanger.

Cookie Projects

When you're making your exchange cookies, don't forget to add the joy! Remember, there will be dozens of cookies on the table—those in the merriest shapes and the coolest colors will be the talk of the party. As you're about to see, any holiday shape you can dream up can become an amazing decorated cookie. All your festive favorites are here! Showers of snowflakes accented with swirls, sugar pearls and snowman faces. Fun ornaments with candy hangers. Jolly elves who stand up to join the party. You can even combine cookies in a sensational scene, such as our village of gingerbread house fronts, each with its own colorful Alpine design. With the easy instructions here and the variety of cutters and toppings on pages 88-95, your cookies will get everyone in the holiday spirit!

Festive Forest

COOKIE
3 Pc. Christmas Trees Cutter Set, Cookie Sheet, Cooling Grid

TIPS
1, 2, 3, 4, 13

COLORS*
Kelly Green, Leaf Green, Christmas Red, Red-Red, Brown, Lemon Yellow, Golden Yellow

RECIPES
Color Flow and Royal Icings, p. 87; Roll-Out Cookies, p. 87

ALSO
Flowerful Medley Sprinkles, Rainbow Nonpareils, Light Green Colored Sugar, Color Flow Mix, Meringue Powder, cornstarch

INSTRUCTIONS
Prepare and roll out dough. Cut trees using cutters from set; cut 1½ x 1 in. easel for each cookie. Bake and cool. For trees with sugar backgrounds, sprinkle on colored sugar before baking; add tip 4 icing zigzag or confetti sprinkles after cooling. For nonpareil tree, cover with tip 13 stars; sprinkle on nonpareils. For trees with color flow backgrounds, outline with tip 2 and full-strength icing; flow in with thinned icing (stars and tree trunks should also be done now with color flow). For versions with flow-in decorations, before background icing has set, use tip 2 to pipe on full-strength color flow polka dots (use assorted colors and sizes), horizontal lines (alternate colors) or zigzags (use 2 colors and swirl with a toothpick). Your decorations will sink and blend right into the background! Let color flow trees dry overnight before adding decorations in royal or color flow icing. We show tip 2 lattice, tip 2 garland, tip 13 stars, tip 1 dots, outlines, starbursts and spirals. Stars and tree trunks can be decorated using tip 2, 3 or 13 icing zigzags or tip 2 to outline and fill in (pat smooth with finger dipped in cornstarch). Attach easel to cookie back with royal icing.

Combine Kelly Green with Leaf Green for green shades shown. Combine Christmas Red with Red-Red for red shown. Combine Lemon Yellow with Golden Yellow for yellow shown. Combine Brown with Red-Red for brown shown.

The Sleigh Team

COOKIE
3 Pc. Holiday Cutter Set, Cookie Sheet, Cooling Grid

TIPS
1, 2, 3

COLORS*
Red-Red, Black, Copper (for skin tone shown), Brown

RECIPES
Royal Icing, Roll-Out Cookies, p. 87

INSTRUCTIONS
Prepare and roll out dough. Cut cookies using cutters from set. Bake and cool. For reindeer, outline nose and antlers with tip 2 and full-strength icing. Let dry. Flow in head, antlers and nose with thinned icing. Let dry overnight. Pipe tip 1 dot eyes, outline mouth and bead inner ears. For Santa, outline hat with tip 2 and full-strength icing. Flow in with thinned icing. Let dry overnight. Ice face area smooth. Pipe tip 3 swirl hat trim and pompom; immediately sprinkle on Sparkling Sugar. Pipe tip 2 dot nose, swirl beard and pull-out bead mustache. Add tip 1 dot eyes and outline mouth.

Combine Brown with Red-Red for brown shades shown.

A Frosty Face

COOKIE
- Round Comfort-Grip Cutter, Cookie Sheet, Cooling Grid

COLOR
Copper (for skin tone shown)

RECIPE
Roll-Out Cookies, p. 87

ALSO
Red and White Candy Melts, White Nonpareils, Cinnamon Drops, Parchment Triangles; shredded coconut (chopped), mini chocolate chips

INSTRUCTIONS
Prepare and tint dough light copper; roll out and cut rounds. Bake and cool. Place cookies on cooling grid set over cookie sheet. Cover top 1½ in. of cookie with melted red candy; let set. Decorate using melted white candy in cut parchment bag. Pipe candy over areas for hat brim and pompom; immediately sprinkle with chopped coconut. Attach chocolate chips for eyes and cinnamon drop for nose. Pipe candy over areas for beard and mustache (leave mouth area open); immediately sprinkle with nonpareils.

These Deer Deliver!

COOKIE
- 12 Pc. Holiday Mini Cutter Set, Cookie Sheet, Cooling Grid

RECIPE
Roll-Out Cookies, p. 87

ALSO
- Light Cocoa (14 oz. covers about 80 to 90 treats), White, Dark Cocoa Candy Melts, Parchment Triangles or Disposable Decorating Bags; Cake Boards; mini pretzels, mini chocolate chips, waxed paper

INSTRUCTIONS
Prepare and roll out dough. Cut heads using bell cutter; trim off clappers with knife. Bake and cool. Melt and mix Light Cocoa candy with some White for a lighter shade of brown. Place cookies on cooling grid over cookie sheet. Cover with melted candy. Chill until set. Cut pretzels for antlers. Position heads on waxed paper-covered board. Using melted candy in cut parchment bag, attach antlers and chocolate chip ears. Pipe outline smile, dot eyes and nose. Chill until set.

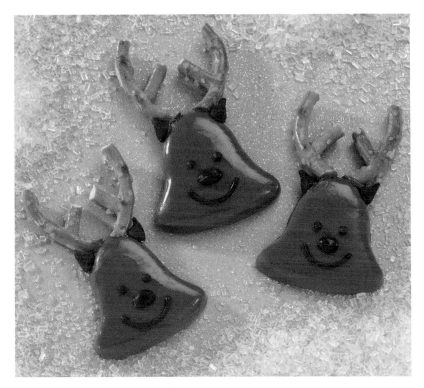

Ever-Great Evergreen

COOKIE
Christmas Cookie Tree Cutter Kit,
Cookie Sheet, Cooling Grid

COLOR
Kelly Green

RECIPES
Color Flow Icing (3 batches),
Roll-Out Cookies, p. 87

ALSO
Color Flow Mix, Light Green
Colored Sugar (2), Piping Gel,
Brush Set,10 in. Cake Circle or
12 in. Cake Plate, Fanci-Foil Wrap,
Parchment Triangles; ⅝ in. wide red
ribbon (11 in. long)

INSTRUCTIONS
Prepare and roll out dough. Cut 2 stars of each
size using cutters from kit. Bake and cool.

Prepare 3 batches of icing; tint 1½ cups dark
green, remainder light green. Outline stars with
full-strength light green icing in cut parchment
bag; let set. Decorate cookies one-at-a-time from
this point. Flow in with thinned light green;
immediately pipe dark green lines from middle of
star to points using cut parchment bag. Pipe lines
in a V-shape from center line. Let dry. Brush
cookie edges with Piping Gel. Cover with light
green sugar. Assemble tree on foil-wrapped board
or cake plate, stacking from largest to smallest
and securing with dots of icing. Make a bow and
attach to treetop with dots of icing.

Potted Poinsettias

COOKIE
Cookie Pro ULTRA II Cookie Press, Cookie Sheet, Cooling Grid

TIPS
2, 3, 352

COLORS
Christmas Red, Kelly Green, Golden Yellow

RECIPES
Royal Icing, p. 87;
Classic Spritz Cookies, p. 86

ALSO
White Ready-To-Use Rolled Fondant (24 oz. makes 12 pots), White Candy Melts, Fanci-Foil Wrap, 8 in. Lollipop Sticks, Meringue Powder, Brush Set, Clear Vanilla Extract; new 2 in. diameter clay pot, jelly spearmint leaves, ⅝ in. wide ribbon (20 in. per pot), 6 in. craft foam square, crushed chocolate cookie crumbs, waxed paper

INSTRUCTIONS
Paint lollipop sticks with a mixture of clear vanilla and green icing color. Push end into craft square and let dry.

Prepare dough. Use flower disk with cookie press to make 6 cookies per pot. Bake and cool. Pipe tip 352 pull-out leaves to form poinsettias. Pipe 8 leaves for bottom row, then 8 shorter leaves on top, positioning tips between tips of bottom row. For centers, pipe 6 tip 3 green dots; overpipe tip 2 yellow dots. Cut spearmint candies in half for thinner leaves. Use melted candy to attach cookies and leaves to painted sticks; chill until set. Wrap pot with 8 x 16 in. piece of Fanci-Foil; secure with ribbon and tie bow. Fill pot with 2 oz. fondant. Insert flowers. Cover fondant with cookie crumbs.

Sparkling Swirls

COOKIE
9 Pc. Holiday Cutter Set, Cookie Sheet, Cooling Grid

TIPS
1, 2

COLORS*
Christmas Red, Red-Red, Leaf Green, Kelly Green

RECIPES
Color Flow Icing, Roll-Out Cookies, p. 87

ALSO
Color Flow Mix, Red and Dark Green Colored Sugar, White Nonpareils, Disposable Decorating Bags

INSTRUCTIONS
Prepare and roll out dough. Cut cookies; bake and cool. Outline tree and bottom part of stocking with tip 2 and full-strength icing; let set. Flow in with thinned icing; let dry. Outline stocking cuff with tip 2 and full-strength icing; let set. Flow in with thinned icing. Let set for 3 to 5 minutes. Sprinkle on nonpareils; let dry. Pipe tip 1 swirl designs using full-strength icing; sprinkle on matching sugars.

Combine Christmas Red with Red-Red for red shown. Combine Leaf Green with Kelly Green for green shown.

Welcome to Winter!

COOKIE
18 Pc. Holiday Cutter Set, Cookie Pro ULTRA II Cookie Press, Comfort-Grip Christmas Tree Cutter, Cookie Sheet, Cooling Grid

TIPS
2, 3, 4, 16

COLORS
Kelly Green, Brown, Christmas Red, Orange, Black

RECIPE
Classic Spritz Cookies, p. 86; Royal Icing, Roll-Out Cookies, p. 87

ALSO
White Candy Melts, 11¾ in. Lollipop Sticks, Jumbo Rainbow Nonpareils, White Nonpareils, Sugar Pearls, Parchment Triangles, Meringue Powder; white curling ribbon, 8 x 2 in. high craft foam circle, cornstarch, 8 in. glass bowl

INSTRUCTIONS
Prepare spritz dough. Use snowflake disk with cookie press to make 8-10 cookies. Bake and cool. Prepare and roll out dough. Cut 3 trees using Comfort-Grip Cutter and cut 1 snowman using cutter from set. Bake and cool. Pipe snowflake points using melted candy in cut parchment bag; immediately sprinkle with white nonpareils. Cover trees with tip 16 stars in royal icing; immediately sprinkle with rainbow nonpareils and let dry. For snowman, ice head and body smooth with royal icing. Outline and pipe in hat and brim with tip 4. Add tip 4 outline hatband, tip 3 dot eyes, buttons, outline mouth and pull-out nose. Pipe tip 4 outline scarf and tails (pat smooth with finger dipped in cornstarch), tip 2 pull-out fringe. Attach all cookies to lollipop sticks with melted candy. Let set. Trim sticks as needed. Insert cookies in craft circle; position ribbon. To display as shown, position craft circle with cookies in glass bowl; fill with Sugar Pearls and position ribbon.

Flaky Friends

COOKIE
4 Pc. Nesting Snowflakes Metal Cutter Set, Cookie Sheet, Cooling Grid

TIPS
2, 3

COLORS
Christmas Red, Kelly Green, Orange, Black

RECIPES
Royal Icing, Chocolate Orange Cut-Outs, p. 87

ALSO
Meringue Powder, Parchment Triangles; waxed paper

INSTRUCTIONS
In advance: Make heads. Using thinned royal icing in a cut parchment bag, pipe 1 in. puddle dots (p. 11) on waxed paper-covered surface. Let dry 24 hours.

Prepare and roll out dough. Cut snowflakes using 2nd smallest cutter from set. Bake and cool. Decorate with full-strength icing. Pipe tip 2 outline snowflake details. Attach heads to center. Using tip 3, outline and pipe in top hat and Santa hat; pipe dot earmuffs, outline headband, zigzag and swirl fur trim on Santa hat. Using tip 2, pipe dot eyes and cheeks; pipe outline mouth and band on top hat. Pipe tip 3 pull-out noses.

Snowmen Stand Tall

COOKIE
12-Cavity Non-Stick Holiday Cookie Shapes Pan, 101 Cookie Cutters, Cookie Sheet, Cooling Grid

TIPS
1, 2, 3, 4, 8, 349

COLORS
Christmas Red, Kelly Green, Orange, Black

RECIPE
Royal Icing, Sugar Cookies (for non-stick pans), p. 87

ALSO
White Sparkling Sugar, Meringue Powder, Disposable Decorating Bags; cornstarch, vegetable pan spray

INSTRUCTIONS
Prepare dough. Press half of dough into pan cavities; bake and cool snowmen. Roll out remaining dough; cut 1 circle base for each treat using medium round cutter from set. Bake and cool. Spatula ice snowman's head and body smooth. Pipe tip 8 outline arms. Outline and pipe in top of hat with tip 4 (pat smooth with finger dipped in cornstarch). Pipe tip 4 outline hat brim. Pipe tip 3 hat band and finger section of mittens (pat smooth). Add tip 3 pull-out thumb. Pipe tip 2 dot eyes and mouth, tip 3 pull-out dot nose. Pipe tip 349 holly leaves on hat; add tip 1 dot berries. Pipe tip 1 pull-out fringe on scarf ends. Let dry overnight. Spatula ice round cookies for fluffy snow. Stand snowman in center; add extra icing for support if necessary. Sprinkle with Sparkling Sugar.

Stylin' Snowmen

COOKIE
18 Pc. Holiday Cutter Set, Cookie Sheet, Cooling Grid

TIPS
2, 3

COLORS
Christmas Red, Black, Kelly Green

RECIPES
Color Flow Icing, p. 87; Roll-Out Cookies, Chocolate Orange Cut-Outs, p. 87

ALSO
Color Flow Mix, White Sparkling Sugar, Parchment Triangles; cornstarch

INSTRUCTIONS
In advance: Prepare and roll out dough. Cut cookies using snowman cutter from set. Bake and cool. Outline with tip 3 and full-strength icing; flow in with thinned icing in cut parchment bag. Let dry overnight.

Decorate with full-strength icing. Outline and pipe in hat with tip 3 (pat smooth with finger dipped in cornstarch). Pipe tip 2 outline hatband, tip 3 outline scarf and bead bowtie with dot knot (pat smooth). Pipe tip 2 outline mouth, dot buttons, eyes, nose and cheeks. Pipe tip 2 c-motion swirls at bottom and immediately sprinkle with Sparkling Sugar.

Custom Cottages

COOKIE
3 Pc. Gingerbread Cutter Set,
Cookie Sheet, Cooling Grid

TIPS
1, 2, 3, 5

RECIPES
Royal Icing, p. 87;
Gingerbread Cookies, p. 86

ALSO
Flowerful Medley Sprinkles, Jumbo
Rainbow Nonpareils, White
Sparkling Sugar, Meringue
Powder, Rolling Pin; spice drops,
granulated sugar, waxed paper,
knife, ruler

INSTRUCTIONS
Prepare and roll out dough. Cut houses using cutter from set. Bake and cool. Decorate in your choice of styles. For candy-trimmed house, use tip 5 to outline and pipe in door and rooftop (pat smooth). Attach confetti to roof and nonpareils around door. Add a single nonpareil for doorknob and confetti for door window. For larger windows, roll out spice drops on waxed paper sprinkled with sugar. Cut ½ in. squares and attach with icing. Add tip 2 outlines. Pipe tip 3 pull-out icicles under roof and windows. Piped house is decorated with tip 1 outlines, spirals and e-motion curls. Sparkling house is decorated using tip 5. Outline and fill in door (pat smooth with finger dipped in cornstarch). Outline window panes; outline and fill in eaves, overpipe door, window frame and immediately sprinkle all with Sparkling Sugar.

Holiday Chalet

COOKIE
3 Pc. Gingerbread Cutter Set,
6 Pc. Holiday Mini Cutter Set,
Cookie Sheet, Cooling Grid

TIPS
1, 2, 3, 5, 6, 16

COLORS*
Kelly Green, Red-Red,
Christmas Red

RECIPES
Royal Icing, p. 87;
Gingerbread Cookies, p. 86

ALSO
Meringue Powder, Jumbo
Confetti Sprinkles, Cinnamon
Drops, Rainbow Nonpareils,
Jumbo Rainbow Nonpareils,
6 and 8 in. Cake Circles,
Fanci-Foil Wrap, Rolling Pin,
Roll & Cut Mat; ruler, knife,
granulated sugar, spice drops,
pinwheel mints, cornstarch,
waxed paper, sugar cones

INSTRUCTIONS
Prepare and roll out dough. Using cutters from sets, cut 2 house fronts and 1 mini boy and girl. Also cut 2 side panels, 1½ x 1⅞ in., 2 roof panels, 2¾ in. square, and 1 circle base using 6 in. cake circle as pattern. Bake and cool. Assemble house with icing and tip 6; let set. Outline and pipe in door using tip 3 (pat smooth with finger dipped in cornstarch). Outline door frame and attach jumbo nonpareils for trim and doorknob. Roll out spice drops on waxed paper sprinkled with granulated sugar. Cut to size for all windows and attach with icing. Outline window frame and panes with tip 2. Attach jumbo nonpareils around front and side windows. Attach cinnamon drops above front window and pinwheel mint above door; attach cinnamon drop in center with dot of icing. Ice roof smooth. Pipe tip 5 lattice lines, attach jumbo nonpareils at line intersections. Attach jumbo confetti on roof peak. Pipe tip 3 icicles on roof and tip 2 icicles under windows. For trees, trim cones to various heights from 3 to 5 in. Beginning at bottom of cone, pipe rows of tip 16 pull-out stars, lightly overlapping each row. Attach rainbow nonpareils. For kids, outline and pipe in clothes with tip 3 (pat smooth). Pipe tip 1 dot eyes and string mouth. Pipe tip 2 swirl hair on girl; add details on dress with tip 2. To display, ice round cookie smooth, position house. Position confetti upright around edge. Attach kids and position trees.

Combine Red-Red with Christmas Red for red shown.

Welcome to Candy Lane

COOKIE
Pre-Baked Gingerbread House Kit
(5.25 x 5.5 x 4.75 in.)

TIPS
2, 5

COLORS
Leaf Green, Kelly Green, Christmas Red, Lemon Yellow

RECIPE
Color Flow Icing, p. 87

ALSO
Color Flow Mix, Round Cut-Outs, White Sparkling Sugar, Red Colored Sugar, Brush Set, Piping Gel, Parchment Triangles; sugar cones, pencil, paper, waxed paper, scissors, candy cane sticks

INSTRUCTIONS

Two days in advance: Make color flow trims. For all, outline shape with tip 2 and full-strength icing; let dry, then flow in with thinned icing in cut parchment bag. Trace circles on paper using medium Cut-Out. On one circle trace small Cut-Out in center for wreath. Cover with waxed paper. For wreath, outline green circle, flow in between circles. For roof peak, outline and pipe in 5 circles. For eaves, outline and pipe in 26 semi-circles ¼ in. wide. For door awning and shutters on 3 back windows, outline and pipe in 8 red rectangles, 1½ x ¾ in. For shutters on front and side windows, outline and pipe in 6 red rectangles, 1 x ½ in. For trim above front window, pipe a ¾ in. puddle dot on waxed paper with thinned icing. For wreath, pipe tip 5 bead bow with outline streamers in full-strength icing; let dry. Reserve remaining full-strength icing.

Assemble house using icing mix and base board from kit, following package instructions. Ice roof smooth. Pipe tip 5 zigzag garlands; cover with Sparkling Sugar. Ice door and window areas smooth; outline with tip 5 and full-strength icing. Add tip 2 dot doorknob. Brush awning, shutters, semi-circles for eaves and wreath with Piping Gel and dip in matching sugar. Attach bow to wreath with dots of icing. Pipe tip 5 swirls on roof peak trims and tip 2 swirl on window trim; dip in red sugar. Pipe tip 5 outline window sills; cover with Sparkling Sugar. Cut candy sticks to fit; brush with Piping Gel, cover with Sparkling Sugar and attach to house corners with icing. Attach remaining trims with icing. For trees, cut cones from 3 to 4½ in. high. Brush with Piping Gel, cover with Sparkling Sugar and position.

Seasonal Sparkle

COOKIE
18 Pc. Holiday Cutter
Set, Cookie Sheet,
Cooling Grid

TIPS
6, 9

RECIPE
Roll-Out Cookies,
p. 87

ALSO
Star Cut-Outs,
Red, Light Green,
Yellow Colored Sugars;
White Sparkling Sugar;
Flowerful Medley &
Jumbo Stars Sprinkles,
Piping Gel, Brush Set,
spice drops, granulated
sugar, mini chocolate
chips, waxed paper,
scissors

INSTRUCTIONS
Prepare and roll out dough. Cut cookie shapes using cutters from set; bake and cool. For all designs except those specified, brush areas with Piping Gel and sprinkle with Colored or Sparkling Sugars. For star, position medium Cut-Out in center; brush center area and cookie edge with Piping Gel and sprinkle with yellow sugar. Brush remaining area with gel and sprinkle with white Sparkling Sugar. For tree, attach confetti sprinkles from Flowerful Medley assortment and jumbo star with Piping Gel. For snowman, leave hat area plain. Roll out spice drops on waxed paper sprinkled with sugar. Cut hat using snowman cutter from set; use scissors to cut a 1½ x ¼ in. strip for scarf and 1 x ¼ in. strips for fringe. Cut buttons with narrow end of tip 9, nose with narrow end of tip 6 and mouth with wide end of tip 6. Attach all pieces, along with mini chocolate chip eyes, with Piping Gel.

Candy-Cookie Combos!

COOKIE
Holiday & Winter
Cookie Candy Molds

CANDY
White, Light Cocoa,
Red Candy Melts
(1 pk. makes about
12 treats), Primary
and Garden Candy
Color Sets

ALSO
Parchment Triangles,
Decorator Brush Set;
round sandwich
cookies (2 in. diameter
or less)

INSTRUCTIONS
Melt and tint portions of candy green, light green, yellow, red, orange, blue and black. Use piping or painting method to fill in mold details. Chill until set. Fill cavities half full using melted candy in background colors; press in cookie. Pipe on additional candy to seal top. Chill until set.

Stocking Up for Christmas

COOKIE
18 Pc. Holiday Cutter Set, Cookie Sheet, Cooling Grid

TIPS
1s, 2, 3, 352

COLORS*
Sky Blue, Violet, Rose, Leaf Green, Lemon Yellow, Orange

RECIPES
Royal Icing, Roll-Out Cookies, p. 87

ALSO
Meringue Powder, Parchment Triangles

INSTRUCTIONS
Prepare and roll out dough. Cut cookies using stocking cutter from set. Bake and cool. Using tip 3, outline cookies with full-strength icing, flow in with thinned icing. For striped design, flow in each section before previous section dries. For other designs, decorate immediately after flowing in stocking using tip 2 for dots, tip 1s for spirals. Let dry overnight.

Using full-strength icing, pipe tip 352 pull-out leaf cuffs. Each serves 1.

*Combine Violet with Rose for violet shown.

The Light Brigade

COOKIE
12 Pc. Holiday Mini Cutter Set, Cookie Sheet, Cooling Grid

TIPS
2, 3

COLORS*
Kelly Green, Christmas Red, Royal Blue, Orange, Lemon Yellow, Golden Yellow, Violet, Rose, Black

RECIPES
Royal Icing, Roll-Out Cookies, p. 87

ALSO
Silver Pearl Dust, Decorating Brush, Meringue Powder, Parchment Triangles

INSTRUCTIONS
Prepare and roll out dough. Cut cookies using ornament cutter from set; trim off top point for threaded straight base. Bake and cool. Using gray for base and colors for bulb, outline cookies with tip 2 and full-strength icing. Flow in with thinned icing. Let dry overnight. Pipe tip 3 lines over base; let dry about 1 hour then brush with Pearl Dust.

*Combine Violet with Rose for violet shown. Combine Lemon Yellow with Golden Yellow for yellow shown.

Tree-Trimming Treats

COOKIE
Christmas Push-N-Print Cutter Set, Cookie Sheet, Cooling Grid

RECIPE
Shortbread (from Push–N-Print package)

ALSO
White, Red, Green, Dark Cocoa Candy Melts, Dessert Accents Candy Mold, Primary Candy Color Set, Parchment Triangles, Sugar Pearls, Rainbow Nonpareils, marshmallows, waxed paper

INSTRUCTIONS
In advance: Mold candy hangers in swirl section of candy mold. Chill until firm. Also: Make caps. Cut marshmallows in half and dip in melted white candy; let set on waxed paper.

Prepare and roll out dough. Cut out cookies and imprint half using 3 disk designs. Bake and cool. Pipe in imprinted cookies using melted candy in cut parchment bags. Attach nonpareils and Sugar Pearls to designs. Sandwich plain and decorated cookies with melted cocoa candy. Attach marshmallow cap to top with melted candy. Attach hangers to marshmallows with melted candy.

Happy Holly-Days!

COOKIE
12 Pc. Holiday Mini Cutter Set, Cookie Sheet, Cooling Grid

TIP
3

COLOR
Kelly Green

RECIPE
Roll-Out Cookies, p. 87

ALSO
Green Candy Melts, Leaf Green Pearl Dust, Brush Set, Parchment Triangles, Cinnamon Drops; lemon extract

INSTRUCTIONS
Prepare and tint dough green; roll out. Use holly leaf cutter to cut 3 leaves for each treat. Thin small amount of dough to piping consistency. Use tip 3 to pipe vein lines. Bake and cool. Brush veins with mixture of Pearl Dust and extract; let dry. Use melted candy in cut parchment bag to attach cookies in groups of three (1 at bottom, 2 on top). Attach Cinnamon Drop berries.

Celestial Caroler

COOKIE
3 Pc. Christmas Trees Cutter Set, Heart and Round Cut-Outs, Cookie Sheet, Cooling Grid

TIPS
2, 3, 7

COLORS*
Brown, Red-Red, Black, Copper (for skin tone shown)

RECIPES
Royal Icing, Roll-Out Cookies, p. 87

ALSO
White Sparkling Sugar, White Pearl Dust, Meringue Powder, Brush Set; round hollow center hard candy, waxed paper, cornstarch

INSTRUCTIONS
Prepare and roll out dough. For each angel, cut 1 tree using triangle tree cutter from set (cut off trunk), 1 circle using medium Cut-Out from set and 2 hearts using medium Cut-Out from set. Bake and cool. Outline cookies with tip 3 and full-strength icing; flow in with thinned icing. Let set for 3 to 5 minutes and then sprinkle hearts with Sparkling Sugar. Let all dry overnight. Assemble angel on waxed paper-covered board. Use icing to attach heart wings behind tree body; attach head to body (use a ball of icing behind top of head for support). Use tip 2 to pipe swirl hair, dot nose, fill-in mouth, outline eyes and S-Scroll trim on dress. Attach hard candy halo. Pipe tip 7 C-motion sleeves, starting at tapered shoulders. Overpipe tip 3 outline hands. Flatten with finger dipped in cornstarch; indent center line with edge of knife. Let dry several hours. Brush dress with white Pearl Dust.

Combine Brown with Red-Red for brown shown.

Angel Chorus

COOKIE
18 Pc. Holiday Cutter Set, Cookie Sheet, Cooling Grid

TIPS
1s, 2, 3

COLORS*
Kelly Green, Rose, Violet, Lemon Yellow, Brown, Red-Red, Copper (for skin tone shown)

RECIPES
Royal Icing, Roll-Out Cookies, p. 87

ALSO
White and Gold Pearl Dust, Meringue Powder, Disposable Decorating Bags, Brush Set; lemon extract, cornstarch

INSTRUCTIONS
Prepare and roll out dough. Cut cookies using angel cutter from set. Bake and cool. Use tip 3 to outline and pipe in head, wing and dress (pat smooth with finger dipped in cornstarch). Use tip 3 to pipe hand and halo. Use tip 2 to pipe swirl hair and outline details on wing and dress. Pipe tip 1s outline eye and mouth. Let dry. Brush wings with white Pearl Dust. Brush halos with mixture of lemon extract and gold Pearl Dust.

Combine Violet with Rose for violet shown. Combine Brown with Red-Red for brown shown.

Golden Gifts

COOKIE
6 Pc. Holiday Mini Cutter Set, 101
Cookie Cutters, Cookie Sheet,
Cooling Grid

TIP
3

COLORS*
Black, Violet, Sky Blue,
Kelly Green

RECIPES
Royal Icing, Roll-Out Cookies, p. 87

ALSO
Gold Pearl Dust, Clear Vanilla
Extract, Meringue Powder,
Parchment Triangles, Brush Set

INSTRUCTIONS
Prepare dough and roll out. Cut circle bases using medium circle cutter
from set and gifts using mini cutter. Bake and cool.

Tint portions of icing violet, green, and blue in both light and dark shades;
reserve some white. Outline circles and gifts using tip 3 and full-strength
icing; let set. Flow in cookies with thinned icing in cut parchment bag.
Immediately pipe small white dots in cut bag; let dry overnight. Using tip 3
and full-strength icing, pipe white ribbons, bows and dot knots on gifts; let
set 15 minutes. Combine Pearl Dust with a little vanilla extract; paint
ribbons and bows. Attach gifts to circles using full-strength royal icing.

*Combine Violet with a little Black for violet shown. Combine Kelly Green with a
little Black for green shown. Combine Sky Blue with Violet for blue shown.*

High-Style Stars

COOKIE
Christmas Cookie Tree Cutter Kit, Cookie Sheet, Cooling Grid

TIPS
2, 3

RECIPES
Royal Icing, Roll-Out Cookies, p. 87

ALSO
Gold and Silver Pearl Dust, Meringue Powder, Brush Set, Candy Melting Plate, Parchment Triangles, Cake Board; waxed paper, lemon extract, tweezers

INSTRUCTIONS
Make puddle dots (p. 11). Using thinned royal icing in cut parchment bag, pipe balls in various sizes on waxed paper. For centers, you will need ½ or ⅝ in. diameter dots. For other dots you will need sizes ranging from ⅛ to 3/16 in. Let dry 48 hours. Brush all dots with a mixture of Pearl Dust and lemon extract. Let dry.

Prepare and roll out dough. Cut stars using 3rd, 4th and 5th smallest cutters from kit; bake and cool. Outline cookies using tip 3 and full-strength icing. Flow in using thinned icing in cut bag; let dry. For dotted design, attach approximately 60 3/16 in. puddle dots with tip 2 dots of icing. Decorate remaining cookies with tip 2 or 3 starburst lines or tip 3 swirls; attach puddle dots; let dry. Brush designs with Pearl Dust/lemon extract mixture; let dry.

Snowflakes & Star Showers

COOKIE
6 pc. Holiday Mini Cutter Set, Cookie Sheet, Cooling Grid

RECIPE
Roll-Out Cookies, p. 87

ALSO
White & Light Cocoa Candy Melts, White Nonpareils, White Sparkling Sugar, Sugar Pearls, Parchment Triangles

INSTRUCTIONS
Prepare dough and roll out. Cut cookies using various cutters from set. Bake and cool. Place cookies on cooling grid over cookie sheet. Cover with melted candy; tap grid to spread evenly and let dry. Using melted candy in cut parchment bag, decorate with outlines, swirls and veins as desired. Add sugars, nonpareils or Sugar Pearls over designs.

Perky Poinsettias

COOKIE
3 Pc. Snowflake Cutter
Set, Cookie Sheet,
Cooling Grid

TIP
2

COLORS
Lemon Yellow, Leaf
Green, Christmas Red

RECIPES
Royal Icing, Roll-Out
Cookies, p. 87

ALSO
White, Ruby Red,
Yellow Pearl Dust,
Brush Set, Meringue
Powder, Parchment
Triangles

INSTRUCTIONS
In advance: Make cookies. Prepare dough
and roll out. Cut cookies using pointed
snowflake cutter; bake and cool. Outline
cookies with tip 2 and full-strength royal
icing; let set. Flow in with thinned royal
icing in cut parchment bag. Let dry
overnight.

For petals, outline and flow in as above;
let dry a few hours or overnight. Pipe tip
2 dots in full-strength royal icing. Brush
petals with matching Pearl Dust.

Hanging Out for the Holidays

COOKIE
18 Pc. Holiday Cutter
Set, 12 Pc. Holiday
Mini Cutter Set, Cookie
Sheet, Cooling Grid

TIPS
1, 2, 3

COLORS*
Christmas Red,
Red-Red, Kelly Green,
Brown

RECIPES
Royal, Color Flow
Icings, Roll-Out
Cookies, p. 87

ALSO
White Sparkling Sugar,
Red and Dark Green
Colored Sugars, White
Nonpareils, Color Flow
Mix, Meringue Powder

INSTRUCTIONS
Prepare and roll out dough. For each
treat, cut 1 stocking using cutter from
18 Pc. Set and 1 candy cane and 1
gingerbread boy using cutters from
12 Pc. Set. For striped stockings, add
colored sugars in alternating colors
before baking. Bake and cool all cookies.
For green stocking, ice smooth with light
shade of royal icing. Add tip 2 lattice
outlines. For red stocking, outline using
tip 3 and full-strength color flow icing;
flow in with thinned color flow. Let dry
overnight, then print tip 2 name. Finish
stockings with your choice of fur trims
in royal icing: fluffy icing swirls, icing
covered with white nonpareils or icing
sprinkled with sparkling sugar. For
gingerbread boys, ice smooth with
brown icing; add tip 1 dot, outline and
pipe-in details. For candy canes, outline
and pipe in stripes in alternating colors.
Attach mini cookies behind stockings
using full-strength color flow icing.

*Combine Christmas Red with Red-Red for
red shown. Combine Brown with Red-Red for
brown shown.

The Greatest Gift

COOKIE
6 Pc. Holiday Mini Cutter Set, Hearts Plastic Nesting Cutter Set, Cookie Sheet, Cooling Grid

TIPS
1, 2, 10

COLORS*
Christmas Red, Red-Red, Leaf Green, Kelly Green, Black

RECIPES
Color Flow Icing, Roll-Out Cookies, p. 87

ALSO
Color Flow Mix, Disposable Decorating Bags; ¼ in. wide ribbon (7 in. for each heart)

INSTRUCTIONS
Prepare and roll out dough. Cut hearts using second largest cutter from set; use narrow end of tip 10 to cut out hole near top. Cut doves using cutter from set. Bake and cool cookies. Outline cookies using tip 2 and full-strength icing; flow in with thinned icing. Let dry. Add details using full-strength icing. Pipe tip 1 message on heart and details on dove. Pipe tip 2 scrolls on heart. Attach dove to heart with icing. Thread ribbon through hole and tie.

*Combine Christmas Red with Red-Red for red shown. Combine Leaf Green with Kelly Green for green shown.

Sparkle Tree

COOKIE
Cookie Pro ULTRA II Cookie Press, 6 Pc. Nesting Stars Metal Cutter Set, Cookie Sheet, Cooling Grid

TIP
6

RECIPES
Classic Spritz Cookies p. 86; Royal Icing, Roll-Out Cookies p. 87

ALSO
Green Candy Melts (3 pks.), Light Green and Yellow Colored Sugars, White Sparkling Sugar, Jumbo Confetti Sprinkles, Meringue Powder;12 in. craft foam cone, pastry brush, self-sealing plastic wrap

INSTRUCTIONS
Prepare spritz dough. Use heart disk with cookie press to make approximately 70 cookies. Prepare and roll out dough; cut star using 2nd smallest nesting cutter. Sprinkle with yellow sugar. Bake and cool all cookies.

Place heart leaf cookies on cooling grid over cookie sheet and cover with melted candy; sprinkle with light green sugar. Chill until firm. Using tip 6 and royal icing, pipe zigzag snow on cookie points; immediately dip in Sparkling Sugar. Let dry.

Ice craft cone smooth with royal icing; cover with plastic wrap. Brush surface of wrap with melted candy and chill until firm. Using melted candy, attach cookie leaves at a 45° angle starting at bottom of cone. Attach jumbo confetti to leaves with dots of melted candy. Attach star cookie with melted candy.

Party Poinsettia

COOKIE
101 Cookie Cutters,
18 Pc. Holiday Cutter
Set, Cookie Sheet,
Cooling Grid

TIP
2

RECIPE
Roll-Out Cookies, p. 87

ALSO
White Ready-To-Use
Decorator Icing, Piping
Gel, Red and Light
Green Colored Sugar,
Brush Set, Fanci-Foil
Wrap, 8 in. Cake
Circles or 10 in. cake
plate; mini candy-
coated chocolates

INSTRUCTIONS
Prepare and roll out dough. Using cutters from sets, cut 12 holly leaves and 1 small round cookie. Bake and cool. Brush tops with Piping Gel; sprinkle with colored sugars. Attach mini chocolates to round cookie with tip 2 dots of icing. Position cookies on foil-wrapped cake circle or cake plate.

Welcoming Wreath

COOKIE
18 Pc. Holiday Cutter
Set, Cookie Sheet,
Cooling Grid

TIP
3

COLOR
Kelly Green

RECIPES
Royal Icing, Roll-Out
Cookies, p. 87

ALSO
Dark Green Colored
Sugar, Meringue
Powder, Cinnamon
Drops, Fanci-Foil
Wrap, 12 in. Cake
Circle or cake plate;
1 in. wide satin ribbon
(24 in.), serving plate

INSTRUCTIONS
Prepare dough, tint green and roll out. Cut 18 to 22 holly leaves using cutter from set. Bake and cool. Decorate 1 cookie at a time. Pipe tip 3 icing scrolls; immediately sprinkle on colored sugar. Let dry. Arrange on plate in 2 layers. Attach cinnamon drops with dots of icing. Tie bow and attach with icing.

December Doves

COOKIE
3 Pc. Winter Cutter Set, Cookie Sheet, Cooling Grid

TIPS
1, 2

COLOR
Royal Blue

RECIPES
Color Flow Icing, Roll-Out Cookies, p. 87

ALSO
White Cake Sparkles; White Sparkling Sugar

INSTRUCTIONS
Prepare dough and roll out. Cut cookies using dove cutter from set; bake and cool. Outline cookies with tip 2 and full-strength color flow; let dry. Flow in with thinned color flow; let dry. Pipe tip 2 dot eye on all cookies. For wings, pipe tip 1 and 2 outlines, dots and swirls. Immediately sprinkle sugar or Cake Sparkles over some wings.

Christmas Place Card Cookies

COOKIE
Christmas Cupcake & Cookie Stencils, Cookie Sheet, Cooling Grid

TIPS
2, 3

COLORS*
Red-Red, Violet, Rose, Kelly Green

RECIPES
Royal Icing, Roll-Out Cookies, p. 87

ALSO
Red, Lavender Colored Sugar, Parchment Triangles, Meringue Powder; ruler, knife

INSTRUCTIONS
In advance: Prepare and roll out dough. Cut 5¼ x 2½ in. rectangles with knife; bake and cool cookies. Using tip 2 and full-strength royal icing, outline cookies. Flow in with thinned icing. Let dry overnight.

Position ornament stencil on cookie and spread with a thin coating of icing. Immediately sprinkle with matching colored sugar. Carefully remove stencil. Pipe tip 3 outline vine and tip 2 name.

Combine Violet with Rose for violet shown.

Santa's Sandwich Cookies

COOKIE
12 Pc. Holiday Mini Cutter Set,
Round Comfort-Grip Cutter,
Cookie Sheet, Cooling Grid

TIP
2

COLORS
Kelly Green, Red-Red

RECIPE
Roll-Out Cookies, p. 87

ALSO
White and Chocolate Tube
Decorating Icings, Coupler Ring
Set, Parchment Triangles; favorite
cookie fillings

INSTRUCTIONS
Prepare and roll out dough. For each cookie, cut 2 rounds; use
assorted mini cutters to cut out center designs on half of cookies.
Thin small amount of cookie dough with water; tint some red for
dots and green for scrolls. Pipe on designs using cut parchment
bags. Bake and cool cookies. Squeeze chocolate tube icing or spread
filling on bottom round cookies; position decorated cookies on top.
For gingerbread boy, pipe dot eyes, buttons and outline smile using
white tube icing and tip 2.

Stacked Sleigh

COOKIE
18 Pc. Holiday Cutter Set, 3 Pc. Holiday Cutter Set, Cookie Sheet, Cooling Grid

TIP
3

COLORS
Royal Blue, Orange, Lemon Yellow, Christmas Red, Kelly Green

RECIPES
Royal Icing, Roll-Out Cookies, p. 87

ALSO
White Nonpareils, Violet, Orange, Blue, Red Colored Sugars, Meringue Powder, Parchment Triangles; candy canes, knife, ruler

INSTRUCTIONS
Prepare dough; tint half green. Roll out and cut gifts in plain dough using cutter from 3 pc. set; sprinkle with colored sugars. Cut sleigh from green dough; use cutter from 18 pc. set for sides (reverse cutter for opposite side). For front, cut a 1⅜ in. square, for back cut a 1⅜ x 1⅝ in. rectangle, for bottom cut a 1⅜ x 2¼ in. rectangle. Bake and cool all cookies.

Assemble sleigh using royal icing; let set. Pipe tip 3 ribbons and bows on gifts; add dot knot. Pipe a tip 3 band of snow on top edge of sleigh, immediately sprinkle with white nonpareils. Cut candy cane runners to fit bottom of sleigh; attach with royal icing. Position gifts.

Toymaker Treats

COOKIE
12 Cavity Non-Stick Holiday Cookie Shapes Pan, 101 Cookie Cutters, Cookie Sheet, Cooling Grid

TIPS
1, 2, 3

COLORS*
Christmas Red, Red-Red, Kelly Green, Royal Blue, Brown, Black, Copper (for skin tone shown)

RECIPES
Royal Icing, Sugar Cookies (for non-stick pans), p. 87

ALSO
Flowerful Medley Sprinkles, Meringue Powder; cornstarch, vegetable pan spray, cone-shaped corn snacks, waxed paper

INSTRUCTIONS
In advance: Prepare hats. Tint enough icing for shirts, pants and hats. Thin a portion to pouring consistency. Stand corn snacks on cooling grid set over cookie sheet; pour icing over to cover. Let dry overnight on a waxed paper covered surface. Reserve remaining icing.

Prepare dough. For each treat, press dough into boy cavity of pan; bake and cool. Roll out remaining dough; cut 1 round base using medium cutter from set and 1 triangular easel support (1 x 1¼ in. high) for each treat. Bake and cool. Spatula ice boy cookies smooth in light copper. Use tip 3 to outline and pipe in light shirt and dark pants (pat smooth with finger dipped in cornstarch). Outline and pipe in bow tie sides with tip 2, shoes with tip 3. Pipe tip 3 outline suspenders (flatten slightly), dot buttons and dot knot on bow tie. Pipe tip 1 dot eyes and outline mouth, tip 2 swirl hair, dot cheeks and pull-out nose and ears. Attach easel support to back; let dry. Position hat and pipe tip 3 swirl fur brim and pompom; let dry. Spatula ice round cookies fluffy. Attach confetti around border using dots of icing. Position elves.

Combine Christmas Red with Red-Red for red shown.

Chimney Chum

COOKIE
18 Pc. Holiday Cutter Set, 3 Pc. Holiday Cutter Set, Cookie Sheet, Cooling Grid

TIPS
2, 3

COLORS
Christmas Red, Kelly Green, Violet, Royal Blue, Copper (for skin tone shown), Black

RECIPES
Royal Icing, Roll-Out Cookies, p. 87

ALSO
Gold Pearl Dust, Brush Set, Parchment Triangles, Meringue Powder, 8 in. Lollipop Sticks, Popcorn Treat Boxes; waxed paper, red and white craft paper, white marking pen, 3 x 2 x 4 in. high craft foam block, lemon extract, glue stick, cornstarch, ruler

INSTRUCTIONS
Prepare dough and roll out cookies. For each treat, cut 4 gifts using cutter from 3 pc. set and 1 Santa using cutter from 18 pc. set. Outline gifts with tip 2 and full-strength icing; let set. Flow in with thinned icing in cut parchment bag. Decorate remaining cookies on waxed paper with full-strength icing. For gifts use tip 3 to pipe in bow, ribbon and dot knot. For Santa, ice face and body smooth (pat smooth with finger dipped in cornstarch). Pipe tip 2 dot facial features, outline belt and buckle. Pipe tip 3 swirl beard and hat trims. Pipe in tip 3 hat and boots (pat smooth). Let dry overnight.

Brush some ribbons and bows with Pearl Dust/lemon extract mixture. Attach lollipop sticks to back of cookies with icing; let dry. Cut craft foam to fit treat box; insert block, then cookies. Attach red paper to treat box with glue stick; draw 1 x 1¾ in. bricks with marking pen. Cut snow top from white paper, 4½ x 1¼ in. Attach with glue stick.

Entertaining Elf

COOKIE
18 Pc. Holiday Cutter Set, Cookie Sheet, Cooling Grid

TIPS
1, 2, 3, 349

COLORS
Copper (for skin tone shown), Christmas Red, Kelly Green, Brown, Black

RECIPES
Color Flow Icing, Roll-Out Cookies, p. 87

ALSO
Color Flow Mix, Cake Boards, White Candy Melts, Parchment Triangles; scissors, waxed paper, candy canes, granulated sugar, jelly spearmint leaves, spice drops, cone-shaped corn snacks

INSTRUCTIONS
Prepare and roll out dough. Cut cookies using snowman cutter from set; trim off hat and round top of head. Bake and cool. Using tip 2, outline cookies with full-strength icing, flow in with thinned icing. For hat, cover corn snack with thinned icing. Let all dry overnight.

Using tip 2 and full-strength icing, pipe string hair, dot eyeballs and outline mouth; add tip 1 dot pupils, tip 3 pull-out nose, dot cheeks and outline suspenders. For ears, pipe tip 349 pull-out leaves. Pipe tip 2 dot buttons. Cut candy canes into 2 in. lengths for arms, 4 in. lengths for legs. Using melted candy in cut parchment bag, attach hat, arms and legs. Using tip 3 and melted candy, pipe zigzag cuffs on hat and pants, ball pompom on hat. For hands, roll out spice drops ¼ in. thick on waxed paper sprinkled with sugar; cut shapes with scissors. Cut shoes from spearmint leaves. Cut openings in each and insert candy canes.

Colorful Caps

COOKIE
3 Pc. Christmas Trees Cutter Set, Cookie Sheet, Cooling Grid

TIPS
3, 7

COLORS*
Kelly Green, Christmas Red, Red-Red

RECIPES
Color Flow Icing, Roll-Out Cookies, p. 87

INSTRUCTIONS
Prepare and roll out dough. Cut cookies using triangle tree cutter from set; cut off trunks. Bake and cool.

Prepare icing and tint portions red, dark and light green; reserve some white. Outline cookies with tip 3 and full-strength icing; let set. For polka dot cookies, flow in with thinned dark green; immediately pipe tip 3 dots in light green. For striped cookies, flow in lines of red and white starting at peak of cap; pipe each section before icing sets. Let dry. With full-strength white icing, pipe tip 7 ball or zigzag trim at bottom and swirl pompom at top.

Combine Christmas Red and Red-Red for red shown.

Holiday Handiwork

COOKIE
3 Pc. Winter Cutter Set, Cookie Sheet, Cooling Grid

TIPS
1, 2, 8

COLORS*
Sky Blue, Royal Blue, Leaf Green, Kelly Green, Christmas Red, Red-Red, Black, Orange

RECIPES
Color Flow Icing, Roll-Out Cookies, p. 87

ALSO
Disposable Decorating Bags, Color Flow Mix, White Nonpareils, White Sparkling Sugar; cornstarch

INSTRUCTIONS
Prepare and roll out dough. Cut mittens using cutter from set; flip cutter to cut opposite hand. Bake and cool. For all designs, outline cuff area with tip 2 and full-strength icing. Flow in with thinned icing. After setting for 3 to 5 minutes sprinkle some with nonpareils or Sparkling Sugar or let area dry and pipe tip 1 swirls in full-strength icing. For color areas, outline with tip 2 and flow in as above. On striped and tree mittens, immediately flow in designs with lighter icing. For snowman, after icing has dried overnight, use full-strength icing to pipe tip 8 ball head and body (pat smooth with finger dipped in cornstarch). Add tip 1 hat, face and scarf details.

Combine Christmas Red with Red-Red for red shades shown. Combine Sky Blue with Royal Blue for blue shown. Combine Leaf Green with Kelly Green for green shades shown.

Snuggled-Up Snowman

COOKIE
Round Cookie Treat Pan, 18 Pc. Holiday Cutter Set, Cookie Sheet, Cooling Grid, 8 in. Cookie Treat Sticks

TIPS
1, 2, 5

COLORS*
Sky Blue, Royal Blue, Black, Orange

FONDANT
Primary Colors Fondant Multi Pack (½ oz. per cookie), Rolling Pin, Roll & Cut Mat, Brush Set

RECIPES
Royal Icing, Roll-Out Cookies, p. 87

ALSO
Meringue Powder; knife, ruler, large marshmallow

INSTRUCTIONS
Prepare and roll out dough. Use Santa Hat cutter from set to cut cookie. For head, press dough in cookie pan; insert stick. Bake and cool cookies. Place round cookie on cooling grid over cookie sheet; cover with thinned royal icing. For hat, pipe stripes using thinned royal icing and tip 2; let set.

Decorate with full-strength icing. Attach hat; let set. Pipe tip 5 swirl pompom and cuff on hat. Pipe tip 2 dot eyes, tip 1 outline mouth, tip 5 pull-out nose and dot cheeks. Cut marshmallow to ½ in. thick; cut in half and wrap around stick for neck. Roll out blue fondant ⅛ in. thick and cut a 3 x ½ in. strip for scarf. Attach around marshmallow with damp brush. For tails, cut 1½ x ½ in. and 2 x ½ in. strips; attach with damp brush. For knot, cut circle with wide end of any tip; attach. Let dry.

Combine Sky Blue and Royal Blue for blue shades shown.

Cool Heads Prevail

COOKIE
Cookie Sheet, Cooling Grid

TIP
3

COLORS
Christmas Red, Kelly Green

RECIPES
Royal Icing, p. 87; Almond Snowballs, p. 84

ALSO
Green, Red and White Candy Melts, White Nonpareils, Meringue Powder, Rolling Pin, Cake Board; waxed paper, granulated sugar, spice drops, mini chocolate chips, cone-shaped corn snacks, paring knife

INSTRUCTIONS
Prepare dough and shape 1 in. balls on cookie sheet; bake and cool. Place cookies on cooling grid over cookie sheet. Cover with melted candy; tap grid to spread evenly and let dry 1-2 minutes. Sprinkle with nonpareils. For eyes, cut tips off chocolate chips and position. For nose, cut a small piece of orange spice drop and roll into a cone; dip in sugar and attach with melted candy. For mouth, roll out black spice drop on waxed paper sprinkled with sugar. Using knife, cut crescent shape and attach with melted candy. For hat, dip corn snack in melted red or green candy; place on waxed paper-covered board and chill until firm. In royal icing, pipe zigzag trim at bottom; let set. Attach to cookie with melted candy; let set. Pipe tip 3 dot or swirl pompom. Each serves 1.

Rooftop Drop-Off

COOKIE
18 Pc. Holiday Cutter Set,
Cookie Sheet, Cooling Grid

TIPS
2, 3, 5

COLORS*
Black, Christmas Red,
Red-Red, Brown, Kelly Green,
Copper (for skin tone shown),
Lemon Yellow, Golden Yellow

RECIPES
Royal Icing, p. 87; Roll-Out
Cookies, Chocolate Orange
Cut-Outs, p. 87

ALSO
Meringue Powder, White
Candy Melts, 11¾ in.
Lollipop Sticks; waxed paper,
3½ x 5½ in. high container,
3 x 4 in. high craft foam
block, wrapping paper, tape,
curling ribbon, 1 in. wide
white ribbon (15 in.), scissors

INSTRUCTIONS
Prepare and roll out dough. Cut 8 chocolate reindeer, 1 each gingerbread boy and sleigh using cutters from set. Bake and cool. For reindeer, outline antlers with tip 3; pipe tip 5 outline harness with tip 2 dots. Using tip 3, pipe dot eyes, pipe in nose and hooves. Add tip 5 pull-out tail. Ice Santa and sleigh smooth. Pipe tip 5 outline runners and swirl trim on sleigh. Position Santa on waxed paper and pipe tip 3 pull-out hat. Pipe tip 3 swirl hair, beard and trim on hat and suit. Pipe tip 3 dot nose, tip 2 dot eyes and mouth. Pipe tip 3 belt, buckle and gloves. Let dry overnight. Attach cookies to lollipop stick with melted candy. Insert craft block in container. Wrap container with wrapping paper. Insert cookies into craft block; trim sticks as needed. Position curling ribbon.

Combine Christmas Red with Red-Red for red shown. Combine Lemon Yellow with Golden Yellow for yellow shown.

Winter Jewels

COOKIE
Comfort-Grip
Snowflake Cutter,
Cookie Sheet,
Cooling Grid

RECIPE
Chocolate Orange
Cut-Outs, p. 87

ALSO
Sugar Pearls, Light
Cocoa Candy Melts
(1 pk. makes about 15
cookies), Parchment
Triangles

INSTRUCTIONS
Prepare and roll out dough. Cut cookies using snowflake cutter; bake and cool. Using melted candy in cut parchment bag, pipe vein lines one section at a time; immediately position Sugar Pearls after piping each section. Let set.

Pearled Presents

COOKIE
18 Pc. Holiday Cutter
Set, Cookie Sheet,
Cooling Grid

TIP
3

COLORS*
Kelly Green, Christmas
Red, Red-Red, Violet,
Rose, Lemon Yellow,
Golden Yellow,
Sky Blue

RECIPES
Color Flow Icing,
Roll-Out Cookies, p. 87

ALSO
Color Flow Mix, White
Pearl Dust, Sugar
Pearls, Brush Set,
Parchment Triangles

INSTRUCTIONS
Prepare and roll out dough. Cut cookies using gift cutter from set. Bake and cool. Prepare icing and tint portions green, red, violet, yellow, and blue; reserve some white. Using tip 3, outline gifts with full-strength icing; flow in with thinned icing. Let dry. Using full-strength white icing with tip 3, pipe in bow. Attach Sugar Pearls to bow area and in desired patterns with dots and lines of icing.

Combine Christmas Red and Red-Red for red shown. Combine Violet and Rose for violet shown. Combine Lemon Yellow and Golden Yellow for yellow shown.

Candy Cane Chain

COOKIE
18 Pc. Holiday Cutter Set,
Cookie Sheet, Cooling Grid

RECIPE
Roll-Out Cookies, p. 87

ALSO
Red, Green and White Candy
Melts, Red and Green Pearlized
Sugars, White Sparkling Sugar,
6-Mix Nonpareils Assortment (red,
green), White Nonpareils, Red,
Green and White Cookie Icing,
Parchment Triangles, Piping Gel,
Brush Set; waxed paper

INSTRUCTIONS
Prepare and roll out dough. Cut candy canes using cutter
from set. Bake and cool. Striped sections for all cookies
will be about ½ in. wide. For sugar and nonpareil
versions, set cookies on waxed paper. Brush piping gel
over areas for colored stripes. Add choice of sprinkles and
use clean, dry brush to even out sprinkles. Repeat for
white stripes. For drizzled Candy Melts and solid Cookie
Icing versions, place cookies on cooling grid set over
cookie sheet. For Candy Melts version, use melted candy
in cut parchment bags. Drizzle on colors first, then white.
For Cookie Icing version, heat icing slightly. Outline and
fill in colors first, then white.

Jolly Gel Cookies

COOKIE
18 Pc. Holiday Cutter Set,
Cookie Sheet, Cooling Grid

RECIPE
Roll-Out Cookies, p. 87

ALSO
White, Red, Green, Yellow Sparkle
Gel, Christmas Nonpareils,
Flowerful Medley Sprinkles, White
Sparkling Sugar

INSTRUCTIONS
Prepare and roll out dough. Cut cookies using cutters
from set; bake and cool. Pipe in sections with Sparkle Gel.
On tree, position confetti from Flowerful Medley
assortment. Sprinkle wreath with nonpareils and hat trim
with Sparkling Sugar.

In Merry Motion

COOKIE
101 Cookie Cutters,
Cookie Sheet,
Cooling Grid

RECIPE
Roll-Out Cookies, p. 87

ALSO
White Candy Melts,
Piping Gel, Brush Set,
White Sparkling Sugar,
Red, Yellow, Dark
Green, Light Green,
Pink, Lavender Colored
Sugars, Rolling Pin,
Parchment Triangles;
zip-close plastic bag

INSTRUCTIONS
Prepare and roll out dough. Cut cookies using smallest round cutter. Sprinkle swirl cookies with white Sparkling Sugar. Bake and cool all cookies. For pinwheels, on waxed paper, trace 4 curving triangle shapes for colored areas; cut out and position on cookie with points meeting in center. Mark triangles with dots of Piping Gel, then fill in with Piping Gel. Sprinkle with Colored Sugar. Place white Sparkling Sugar in zip-close bag; crush fine with rolling pin. Brush open areas with Piping Gel and sprinkle with sugar. For swirls, pipe design with melted candy in cut parchment bag; immediately sprinkle with colored sugar and gently shake to remove excess.

Gingerbread Village

COOKIE
6-Cavity Gingerbread Village Non-Stick Cookie Pan, Cookie Sheet, Cooling Grid

TIPS
1, 2, 3, 4, 6, 8, 16, 349

COLORS
Christmas Red, Kelly Green, Lemon Yellow

RECIPE
Royal Icing, p. 87

ALSO
Gingerbread Mix, Meringue Powder, Jumbo Rainbow Nonpareils Sprinkles, Rainbow Nonpareils, Christmas Nonpareils, Christmas Confetti Sprinkles, Flowerful Medley Sprinkles (Confetti used), Disposable Decorating Bags, jelly spearmint leaves, sugar cones, confectioners' sugar, sifter, waxed paper

INSTRUCTIONS
Prepare Gingerbread Mix and press dough into pan cavities; reserve some dough for easels. Bake and cool cookies following pan directions. Roll out remaining dough on cookie sheet; bake and cool. Cut two 1 x 2 in. rectangle easels for each house. After decorating houses, attach easels to back with royal icing.

Houses can be decorated with any of the following details:

Roof: Outline and pipe in with tip 6. For rounded look, outline with scallop motion, then pipe in. For dormer, leave open area in center; pipe tip 8 dormer roof. Pipe pull-out icicles with tip 3. Pipe ball trims with tip 6 or 8; add spirals with tip 2. Pipe tip 6 zigzag snow on chimney. Attach nonpareils, confetti or sprinkles as desired.

Doors & Windows: Outline wide door frames with tip 6, thinner frames with tip 3 or 4. Door may be piped in with same tip or left plain. Add tip 3 dot doorknob or trims around frame. Outline and pipe in windows with tip 3 or 4; add windowpanes or lattice with tip 2 or 3. Attach nonpareils or sprinkles as desired.

Other details. For candy canes, pipe tip 6 outlines; add spiral lines with tip 1 or 2. For door window or dots at base, pipe balls with tip 6 or 8; add spiral with tip 1 or 2. For holly, pipe tip 349 leaves; attach jumbo nonpareils for berries. For trees, cut sugar cones to various heights (moisten wide end, then cut with scissors to prevent breakage). On waxed paper, pipe tip 16 pull-out branches beginning at base and ending at top. Attach jumbo rainbow nonpareils and dust with sifted confectioners' sugar; let dry. Position around houses.

A Fine Pine

COOKIE
Christmas Cookie Tree Cutter Set, Cookie Sheet, Cooling Grid

COLOR
Kelly Green

RECIPE
Roll-Out Cookies, p. 87

ALSO
Cordial Cups Candy Mold, Light Cocoa Candy Melts, Light Green, Yellow Colored Sugars, Flowerful Medley Sprinkles, Piping Gel, Brush Set, Parchment Triangles

INSTRUCTIONS
Mold bases. Use Cordial Cups mold to make 1 solid candy cup for each tree. Chill until firm.

Prepare dough. Roll out small amount for yellow stars (1 per tree); cut using smallest cutter from set. Tint remaining dough green. For each tree, cut 2 stars with each of the 4 smallest cutters from set. Bake and cool. Brush cookies with Piping Gel; sprinkle with green or yellow sugar. Assemble tree using melted candy in cut parchment bag. Attach confetti trims with melted candy.

North Pole Natives

COOKIE
3 Pc. Holiday Cutter Set, 18 Pc. Holiday Cutter Set, 101 Cookie Cutters, Cookie Sheet, Cooling Grid

TIPS
2, 3, 5, 8, 349

COLORS*
Brown, Red-Red, Copper (for skin tone shown), Christmas Red, Lemon Yellow, Golden Yellow, Black

RECIPES
Royal Icing, Roll-Out Cookies, p. 87

ALSO
White Candy Melts, Meringue Powder; spice drops, red licorice twists, granulated sugar, waxed paper, knife

INSTRUCTIONS
Prepare and roll out dough. For each reindeer cut 1 bell body and 1 head; trim clapper off bell. For each Santa cut 1 head, and 1 medium round body. Bake and cool. Ice cookies smooth. For reindeer, use tip 3 to pipe in antlers, inside ears and nose. Pipe tip 2 dot eyes, outline mouth, tip 5 bead tuft of fur. Pipe tip 8 outline legs and tip 3 hooves. For Santa, pipe tip 5 outline belt and buckle, zigzag trim on suit and hat. Pipe tip 2 dot eyes and mouth, tip 3 dot nose. Pipe tip 3 swirl beard, moustache and pompom. For arms and legs, cut 1½ in. lengths of licorice. For gloves and boots, roll out spice drops on waxed paper sprinkled with sugar; cut shapes with knife and attach to licorice with icing. Pipe tip 3 zigzag cuffs. Attach heads to bodies and Santa arms and legs with melted candy.

Combine Brown and Red-Red for brown shown. Combine Christmas Red with Red-Red for red shown. Combine Lemon Yellow and Golden Yellow for yellow shown.

Toy Soldier

COOKIE
18 Pc. Holiday Cutter Set, Cookie Sheet, Cooling Grid

TIPS
2, 3, 5, 13, 102

COLORS*
Christmas Red, Red-Red, Black, Rose, Golden Yellow, Lemon Yellow, Copper (for skin tone shown)

RECIPES
Royal Icing, Roll-Out Cookies, p. 87

ALSO
Meringue Powder, cornstarch

INSTRUCTIONS
Prepare and roll out dough. Cut cookies using bell cutter from set. Use knife to cut off clapper; bake and cool. Ice face area smooth. Outline top of hat with tip 3; fill in with tip 13 stars. Outline and pipe in hat band with tip 5 (pat smooth with fingertip dipped in cornstarch). Use tip 102 to pipe curved brim. Pipe center fleurs de lis with tip 5 beads and a top dot. Add tip 2 facial features and tip 3 dot cheeks.

Combine Christmas Red with Red-Red for red shown. Combine GoldenYellow with Lemon Yellow for yellow shown.

Cookie Recipes

At a cookie exchange, you'll pick up more than just wonderful treats. You'll also take home great recipes you can use to make your holidays special for years to come. What delicious discovery will you bring to the table? This section is the ideal place to find that new taste sensation! We asked Wilton employees to share the cookies they love most (along with their holiday cookie memories) in our Family Favorite Cookie Contest. Wait until you taste the winning entries...crispy shortbread stars, spicy peppernuts cookies, melt-in-your-mouth almond snowballs and more. You'll also find exciting flavors from the Wilton Test Kitchen, including cool Crème de Menthe Bars, Cocoa-Pecan Meringues and Triple Chocolate Biscotti. They just might win you an award from your fellow bakers!

Cranberry Chocolate Bars

INGREDIENTS

1½ cups all-purpose flour

1¼ teaspoons baking powder

¼ teaspoon salt

1¼ cups (2½ sticks) butter or
    margarine, softened

¾ cup granulated sugar

½ cup firmly-packed brown sugar

2 eggs

2 teaspoons Wilton Pure
    Vanilla Extract

1½ tablespoons orange zest

2¼ cups uncooked quick oats

2 cups semi-sweet chocolate chips

1¼ cups coarsely chopped fresh or
    dried* cranberries

½ cup chopped pecans

¼ cup additional chocolate chips,
    melted (optional)

INSTRUCTIONS

Preheat oven to 325°F. Lightly spray 10 x 15 in. cookie pan with vegetable pan spray.

In small bowl, combine flour, baking powder and salt. In large bowl, beat butter and sugars with electric mixer until light and fluffy. Add eggs and vanilla; mix well. Add flour mixture and orange zest; mix well. Stir in oats, chocolate chips and cranberries. Spread into prepared pan. Top with pecans.

Bake 30-35 minutes or until edges are light golden brown. Cool completely in pan on cooling grid. If desired, drizzle with melted chocolate. Cut into bars.

Makes about 48 bars.

If using dried cranberries, soak in hot water 10-15 minutes to soften before adding to cookie dough. Drain before use.

Apricot Crumble Shortbread Bars

INGREDIENTS

- 3½ cups all-purpose flour
- 2 cups coarsely chopped walnuts
- ½ cup granulated sugar
- ½ cup firmly-packed brown sugar
- 1 teaspoon baking powder
- ¼ teaspoon salt
- 1 cup (2 sticks) butter or margarine, softened
- 1 cup apricot preserves
- 1 cup finely chopped dried apricots

INSTRUCTIONS

Preheat oven to 350°F.

In large bowl, combine flour, walnuts, granulated sugar, brown sugar, baking powder and salt. Cut butter into ½ in. pieces. Add butter to dry ingredients; mix with electric mixer until crumbly, 1 to 2 minutes. Set aside 2 cups of the mixture; press remaining onto bottom of ungreased 11 x 15 in. pan.

Bake 14-16 minutes or until edges are golden brown. In small bowl, combine preserves and dried apricots. Spread mixture over prebaked crust. Sprinkle reserved crumb mixture over surface. Bake an additional 14-16 minutes or until preserves are bubbling and topping is just beginning to brown. Cool completely in pan on cooling grid before cutting.

Makes about 36 bars.

Butterscotch Chocolate Pecan Bars

INGREDIENTS

- 2 cups all-purpose flour
- 1¾ cups firmly-packed light brown sugar, divided
- 1¼ cups (2½ sticks) butter, divided
- 2 cups chopped pecans, divided
- 1 cup butterscotch chips
- 1 cup semi-sweet chocolate chips

INSTRUCTIONS

Preheat oven to 350°F. Lightly spray 13 x 9 in. pan with vegetable pan spray.

In medium bowl, mix flour, 1 cup brown sugar and ½ cup butter with electric mixer at low speed until butter is in small pieces and mixture is crumbly. Press into bottom of prepared pan. Sprinkle with 1½ cups pecan pieces; set aside.

In medium saucepan, combine remaining ¾ cup brown sugar and remaining ¾ cup butter; stir constantly over medium heat until mixture comes to a boil. Continue boiling 1 minute, stirring constantly. Remove pan from heat; carefully pour mixture evenly over pecans and crust.

Bake 18-20 minutes or until bubbly and golden brown. Remove pan from oven; immediately sprinkle with butterscotch and chocolate chips. Let stand 4-5 minutes; spread melted chips, creating a marbled look. Sprinkle with remaining ½ cup pecans, pressing lightly into chocolate. Cool completely.

Makes about 24 bars.

Grandma's Mincemeat Bars

INGREDIENTS

3 eggs
1¼ cups all-purpose flour
1 teaspoon baking powder
⅛ teaspoon salt
1 cup granulated sugar
1 cup jarred or canned mincemeat
1 cup chopped walnuts or pecans
Confectioners' sugar

INSTRUCTIONS

Preheat oven to 300°F. Line 13 x 9 in. pan with parchment paper, allowing excess paper to come up and over sides of pan.

In large bowl, combine eggs, flour, baking powder and salt; mix well (batter will be thick). Add sugar; mix until smooth. Fold in mincemeat and nuts. Spread batter evenly into prepared pan.

Bake 28-30 minutes or until top is golden brown and cake tester inserted in center comes out with moist crumbs. Remove from oven; cool in pan 10 minutes. Lift bars from pan; cool completely. Sprinkle with confectioners' sugar. Cut into bars.

Makes about 5 dozen thin bars.

RECIPE CONTRIBUTED BY

MARY GAVENDA, Senior Cake Decorator

"At my first cookie exchange, one of the young ladies didn't know about Christmas and many traditions that we take for granted others know about. We explained to each other what our Christmas traditions were and she explained what Hanukkah and its history was. I'll always remember that special night when two traditions came together."

Raspberry Bars

INGREDIENTS

1 cup (2 sticks) butter, softened
1 cup granulated sugar
1 egg
3 cups all-purpose flour
1 cup finely chopped pecans
¾ cup raspberry preserves or seedless raspberry jam

INSTRUCTIONS

Preheat oven to 350°F.

In large bowl, beat butter and sugar with electric mixer until light and fluffy. Add egg; mix well. Add flour and pecans; beat at low speed scraping down sides often, until mixture is crumbly. Set aside 1 cup of the mixture; press remaining into bottom of ungreased 9 x 2 in. square baking pan. Spread preserves to within ¼ in. of edge. Sprinkle with reserved crumb mixture.

Bake 40-45 minutes or until preserves are bubbling and topping is golden brown; cool completely. If desired, trim edges before cutting into bars.

Makes about 24 bars.

RECIPE CONTRIBUTED BY

SUE MATUSIAK, Senior Cake Decorator

"No matter if I bake these bars for a cookie exchange, a pot luck or take as a dessert, everyone always says "these are my favorite". What I love is that these bars are so easy to make!"

Triple Chocolate Biscotti

INGREDIENTS

1¼ cups all-purpose flour
½ cup granulated sugar
⅓ cup unsweetened cocoa powder
1½ teaspoons baking powder
¼ teaspoon baking soda
¼ teaspoon salt
2 eggs, lightly beaten
¼ cup (½ stick) butter, melted
1 teaspoon vanilla extract
½ cup white chocolate chips
½ cup milk chocolate chips

INSTRUCTIONS

Preheat oven to 350°F. Line cookie sheet with parchment paper.

In large bowl, combine flour, sugar, cocoa powder, baking powder, baking soda and salt; mix well. In small bowl, combine eggs, butter and vanilla. With electric mixer on low speed, gradually add egg mixture to flour mixture; mix until well blended. Stir in ½ cup white chocolate and milk chocolate chips. On lightly floured work surface, knead dough until smooth. Roll into a 12 in. log; place in middle of prepared cookie sheet.

Bake 25-28 minutes or until firm to the touch. Cool log 30 minutes on cookie sheet. Slice into ½ in. thick pieces. Place slices cut side up on cookie sheet. Reduce oven temperature to 300°F. Bake cut biscotti an additional 15-20 minutes or until firm. Cool 10 minutes on cookie sheet; remove to cooling grid to cool completely.

Makes about 2 dozen biscotti.

Hazelnut Biscotti

INGREDIENTS

1½ cups all-purpose flour
1 teaspoon baking powder
¾ cup finely chopped hazelnuts + additional for garnish
3 eggs
1 cup granulated sugar
½ teaspoon Wilton Clear Vanilla Extract
1 package (14 oz.) Wilton Dark Cocoa Candy Melts

INSTRUCTIONS

Preheat oven to 325°F. Line cookie sheets with parchment paper.

In medium bowl, combine flour, baking powder and ¾ cup hazelnuts. In large bowl, beat eggs and sugar with electric mixer until very light (eggs will be nearly white). Stir in vanilla. Gently fold flour mixture into eggs. Spread dough into 2 long strips on prepared cookie sheet.

Bake 25-30 minutes or until firm and lightly browned. Remove to cooling grid; cool completely. Cut into 1 in. slices; place slices on cookie sheet, cut side up. Return to oven and bake 7-8 minutes. Turn and continue baking until dry about 7-8 minutes. Cool completely on cooling grid.

Melt Candy Melts following package instructions. Dip one end of cooled biscotti in melted candy. Place dipped cookies on parchment-lined cookie sheet; sprinkle with chopped hazelnuts. Chill to set.

Makes about 2 dozen.

Crème de Menthe Bars

INGREDIENTS
- 2 cups chocolate or chocolate mint sandwich cookie crumbs (about 20 cookies)
- 1 package (8 oz.) cream cheese, softened
- ½ cup confectioners' sugar
- 1 can (14 oz.) sweetened condensed milk
- 1 egg
- 2-3 drops Wilton Crème De Menthe Candy Flavoring
- Wilton Kelly Green Icing Color, as desired

Ganache Topping:
- ½ cup heavy whipping cream
- 1 package (14 oz.) Wilton Dark Cocoa Candy Melts, chopped

INSTRUCTIONS
Preheat oven to 325°F. Spray 13 x 9 in. pan with vegetable pan spray. Spread cookie crumbs evenly onto bottom of pan, pressing firmly into pan. Bake 10 minutes. Remove from oven; cool on cooling grid.

In medium bowl, beat cream cheese and sugar with electric mixer until smooth and creamy. In small bowl, combine condensed milk and egg. Gradually add to cream cheese mixture while beating on low speed. Add candy flavoring and icing color; blend well. Pour over cookie crust.

Bake 15-20 minutes or until filling is firm and lightly brown around edges. Cool completely in pan on cooling grid.

Meanwhile, prepare ganache topping. In large saucepan, heat cream (do not boil). Remove from heat; add chopped candy and stir until melted and smooth. Pour over bars; carefully spread to cover evenly. Chill bars until ready to serve. Cut into pieces. Keep refrigerated until ready to serve.

Makes about 32 bars.

Cappuccino Spice Chocolate Chip Cookies

INGREDIENTS
- 5 teaspoons instant coffee
- 2 teaspoons Wilton Clear Vanilla Extract
- 2½ cups all-purpose flour
- 1 teaspoon baking soda
- ¾ teaspoon ground cinnamon
- ¼ teaspoon salt
- 1 cup (2 sticks) butter, softened
- ¾ cup firmly-packed brown sugar
- ¾ cup granulated sugar
- 2 eggs
- 2 cups milk chocolate chips

INSTRUCTIONS
Preheat oven to 350°F. Line cookie sheet with parchment paper.

Dissolve coffee granules in vanilla; set aside. In medium bowl, combine flour, baking soda, cinnamon and salt. In large bowl, beat butter and sugars with electric mixer until light and fluffy. Add eggs and coffee mixture; mix well. Add flour mixture to butter mixture, mixing until just combined. Stir in chocolate chips. Drop by tablespoonfuls onto prepared sheet, about 2 in. apart.

Bake 12-14 minutes or until edges begin to brown. Remove from oven; cool cookies on pan 3 minutes. Remove to cooling grid; cool completely.

Makes about 3 dozen cookies.

Mint Surprise Cookies

INGREDIENTS

2¼ cups all-purpose flour

½ teaspoon baking soda

½ teaspoon salt

¾ cup (1½ sticks) unsalted butter, melted and cooled

¾ cup firmly-packed brown sugar

½ cup granulated sugar

1 egg

1 egg yolk

2 teaspoons Wilton Pure Vanilla Extract

40-50 Wilton Dark Cocoa Mint Candy Melts

Additional Wilton Dark Cocoa Candy Melts, melted (optional)

INSTRUCTIONS

Preheat oven to 375°F. Line cookie sheets with parchment paper.

In medium bowl, combine flour, baking soda and salt. In large bowl, beat butter and sugars with electric mixer until light and fluffy. Add egg, yolk and vanilla; mix well. Add flour mixture; stir until just combined. Roll dough into 1 in. balls; press one Candy Melt into center of each ball, shaping dough around candy to cover completely. Place cookies 2 in. apart on cookie sheets.

Bake 9-11 minutes or until edges are golden brown. Remove cookies to cooling grid; cool completely. If desired, place on parchment paper. Drizzle cookies with additional melted candy, and chill until set.

Makes about 4 dozen cookies.

RECIPE CONTRIBUTED BY

CARMELLA MARKETT, Inside Sales Associate

"I made up this recipe a few years ago when I was making chocolate chip cookies and did not have the bag of chips at home. I substituted Dark Cocoa Mint Candy Melts and my family loved them."

Pecan Tassies

INGREDIENTS

2 refrigerated pie crusts (9 in.)

¾ cup firmly-packed brown sugar

1 tablespoon butter, melted

1 egg, slightly beaten

¼ teaspoon Wilton Pure Vanilla Extract

Pinch of salt

¼ cup chopped pecans

INSTRUCTIONS

Preheat oven to 400°F. Lightly spray mini muffin pan with vegetable pan spray.

Roll out pie crusts ⅛ in. thick (about 12 in. across). Cut 2 in. circles; press into bottom and up sides of prepared pan cavities. In small bowl, combine sugar, butter, egg, vanilla and salt; mix well. Stir in pecans. Spoon 1 teaspoonful of mixture into pie crusts.

Bake 15-20 minutes or until pastry is golden brown. Cool 5 minutes in pan. Remove to cooling grid; cool completely.

Makes about 2½ dozen cookies.

Pecan Sandies

INGREDIENTS

- 1 cup (2 sticks) butter, softened
- ⅔ cup confectioners' sugar
- 2 teaspoons Wilton Pure Vanilla Extract
- 2¼ cups all-purpose flour
- ⅛ teaspoon salt
- ½ cup chopped pecans
- Pecan halves

INSTRUCTIONS

Preheat oven to 325°F.

In large bowl, beat butter and sugar with electric mixer until light and fluffy; add vanilla. Add 2 cups flour, one cup at time, and salt; mix until dough is smooth. If dough feels sticky, add additional ¼ cup flour, as needed. Stir in chopped pecans. Drop by tablespoonfuls onto ungreased cookie sheet; press pecan half onto dough.

Bake 10-12 minutes or until lightly browned. Cool on pan 1-2 minutes. Remove to cooling grid; cool completely.

Makes about 3½ dozen cookies.

Cinnamon Tea Cakes

INGREDIENTS

2 cups all-purpose flour
1 teaspoon ground cinnamon, divided
¼ teaspoon salt
1 cup (2 sticks) unsalted butter, softened
1½ cups confectioners' sugar, divided
1 teaspoon Wilton Pure Vanilla Extract

INSTRUCTIONS

Preheat oven to 375°F. Line cookie sheets with parchment paper.

In small bowl, combine flour, ½ teaspoon cinnamon and salt. In large bowl, beat butter, ¾ cup sugar and vanilla until light and fluffy. Add flour mixture; mix only until combined. Drop by tablespoonfuls onto prepared cookie sheets, placing 2 in. apart.

Bake 8-10 minutes or until bottoms are golden brown. Remove to cooling grid; cool 5 minutes. Combine remaining ¾ cup sugar with remaining ½ teaspoon cinnamon. Roll warm cookies in sugar mixture; cool completely.

Makes about 3 dozen cookies.

RECIPE CONTRIBUTED BY
CARMELLA MARKETT, Inside Sales Associate

"This is an easy recipe that has been around my family for years. Everyone has all the ingredients on hand and they are finished quickly. I've used them for cookie exchanges and colored the dough green using Wilton Icing Color."

Saint Nicholas Cookies

INGREDIENTS
1¾ cups all-purpose flour
½ cup finely ground almonds
¼ teaspoon salt
¾ cup (1½ sticks) butter, softened
½ cup granulated sugar
1 packet (.32 oz.) vanilla sugar
2 egg yolks
½ cup dried currants
½ cup finely chopped mixed dried or candied fruit

INSTRUCTIONS

Preheat oven to 350°F. Line cookie sheet with parchment.

In medium bowl, combine flour, almonds and salt. In large bowl, beat butter, granulated sugar and vanilla sugar with electric mixer until well blended. Add egg yolks; beat until light and fluffy, about 2 minutes. Add flour mixture to butter mixture, mixing just until combined. Stir in fruit. Drop by heaping tablespoonfuls onto prepared sheets, about 1 in. apart.

Bake 8-10 minutes or until bottoms of cookies begin to brown. Remove from oven; cool 3 minutes. Remove to cooling grid; cool completely.

Makes about 4 dozen cookies.

RECIPE CONTRIBUTED BY
GIULIA TARASZKIEWICZ, Associate Product Manager

"Oh—what a wonderful smell is coming from the kitchen! I am upstairs watching TV with my brother and Grandma and Mom are downstairs baking on a snowy afternoon. We jump up and run to the kitchen... Grandma and Mom smile as if they knew this was going to happen. It is the cookie that brings me back to the best family moments ever."

Peanut Butter Kiss Cookies

INGREDIENTS

3 cups all-purpose flour
1 teaspoon baking soda
¼ teaspoon salt
1 cup solid vegetable shortening
1 cup creamy peanut butter
¾ cup granulated sugar
1 cup firmly-packed brown sugar
2 eggs
1 teaspoon Wilton Pure Vanilla Extract
1 package (13 oz.) bite-size chocolate or dark and white chocolate swirl candies

INSTRUCTIONS

Preheat oven to 325°F.

In medium bowl, combine flour, baking soda and salt. In large bowl, beat shortening and peanut butter with electric mixer until light and fluffy. Add sugars; mix well. Add eggs, one at a time, and vanilla, mixing until smooth. Add to shortening mixture; mix well. Roll dough into 1 in. balls (dough will be slightly dry). Place on ungreased cookie pan about 1½ in. apart. With finger, make a depression about ½ in. deep in center of each ball (dough will crack around edges).

Bake 10-12 minutes or until lightly browned. Remove from oven and immediately place 1 candy onto each cookie. Remove from pan to cooling grid; cool completely.

Makes about 5 dozen cookies.

White Chocolate Oatmeal Pistachio Cookies

INGREDIENTS

2 cups all-purpose flour
1 teaspoon baking soda
½ teaspoon salt
1 cup (2 sticks) butter, softened
1 cup firmly-packed brown sugar
½ cup granulated sugar
2 eggs
½ teaspoon Wilton Pure Vanilla Extract
½ teaspoon Wilton No-Color Almond Extract
2 cups uncooked old-fashioned oats
1 package (12 oz.) white chocolate chips
¾ cup chopped pistachios

INSTRUCTIONS

Preheat oven to 350°F.

In medium bowl, combine flour, baking soda and salt. In large bowl, beat butter and sugars with electric mixer until light and fluffy. Add eggs, one at a time, mixing well. Add extracts; blend well. Stir in flour mixture just until combined. Stir in oats, white chocolate chips and pistachios. Spoon heaping tablespoonfuls of dough onto ungreased cookie sheet, about 1 in. apart.

Bake 16 to 18 minutes or until light golden brown. Cool 5 minutes on pan. Remove to cooling grid; cool completely.

Makes about 3½ dozen cookies.

Noah Bedoahs

INGREDIENTS
- 1 ¾ cups all-purpose flour
- ½ teaspoon baking powder
- ¼ teaspoon salt
- 1 cup (2 sticks) unsalted butter; softened
- ½ cup granulated sugar
- ¾ cup mini semi-sweet chocolate chips
- ½ cup finely chopped pecans or walnuts

INSTRUCTIONS
Preheat oven to 275°F. Line cookie sheet with parchment paper.

In medium bowl, combine flour, baking powder and salt. In large bowl, beat butter and sugar with electric mixer until light and fluffy. Add flour mixture to butter mixture; mix until fluffy. Stir in chocolate chips and nuts. Measure generous rounded tablespoons of dough; place on prepared cookie sheets, about 2 in. apart. Press to flatten slightly.

Bake 60 minutes or until just slightly browned on edges. Remove from oven; cool 3 minutes. Remove to cooling grid; cool completely.

Makes about 2 dozen cookies.

Note: These cookies are baked at a low temperature for a full hour to develop flavor and extra crunch.

RECIPE CONTRIBUTED BY
SANDY FOLSOM, Director, The Wilton School of Cake Decorating and Confectionery Art
"The most delicate cookie you have ever tasted."

Peppernuts Cookies

INGREDIENTS
- 3 ¼ cups all-purpose flour
- 2 tablespoons ground cinnamon
- 1 teaspoon baking powder
- 1 teaspoon ground cloves*
- ½ teaspoon salt
- ½ teaspoon ground ginger
- ¼ teaspoon ground allspice
- ¼ teaspoon ground nutmeg
- ⅛ teaspoon ground black pepper
- 3 cups firmly-packed brown sugar
- 4 eggs

INSTRUCTIONS
Preheat oven to 325°F. Line cookie pans with parchment paper.

In large bowl, combine flour, cinnamon, baking powder, cloves, salt, ginger, allspice, nutmeg and black pepper; set aside. In second large bowl, combine brown sugar and eggs; mix well. Add dry ingredients slowly to egg mixture, forming a soft dough. Roll dough into logs about ½ in. thick (about the thickness of a pencil). Cut dough crosswise into ¼ in. pieces (about the size of a peanut). Sprinkle dough pieces onto prepared cookie pans; separate any stuck together.

Bake 12-14 minutes or until golden brown. Cool completely. Cookies will become crunchy as they cool. Break apart any cookies that have baked together. Store in airtight containers.

Makes about 12 cups.

* If desired, increase ground cloves to 1 tablespoon for a more traditional, spicier flavor.

RECIPE CONTRIBUTED BY
CHRISTINA DITTMER, Web Designer
"My grandmother would make this recipe for the family when we all got together for the holidays. She still has the original recipe card with her mother's handwriting on it. She has now passed it on to me."

Snickerdoodles

INGREDIENTS

- 2¾ cups sifted all-purpose flour
- 2 teaspoons cream of tartar
- 1 teaspoon baking soda
- ¼ teaspoon salt
- ½ cup solid vegetable shortening
- ½ cup (1 stick) butter, softened
- 1¾ cups granulated sugar, divided
- 2 eggs
- 1 teaspoon Wilton Pure Vanilla Extract
- 2 teaspoons ground cinnamon

INSTRUCTIONS

Preheat oven to 375°F. Line cookie sheets with parchment paper.

In medium bowl, stir together flour, cream of tartar, baking soda and salt; set aside. In large bowl, beat shortening, butter and 1½ cups sugar until light and fluffy. Add eggs and vanilla; mix well. Add flour mixture to the shortening mixture; mix only until incorporated. Roll dough into 1 in. balls. In small bowl, combine remaining ¼ cup sugar and cinnamon; roll balls in mixture to coat and place 2 in. apart on prepared cookie sheet.

Bake 8-10 minutes or until lightly browned, but still soft. Cool 3 minutes on pan. Remove to cooling grid; cool completely.

Makes about 3 dozen cookies.

Peppermint Ribbon Cookies

INGREDIENTS

- 3 cups all-purpose flour
- 1 teaspoon salt
- ½ teaspoon baking powder
- 1 cup (2 sticks) butter, softened
- 1⅓ cups granulated sugar
- 2 eggs
- 2 teaspoons Wilton Pure Vanilla Extract
- 2 to 4 drops Wilton Peppermint Candy Flavoring
- Wilton Christmas Red Icing Color, as desired
- Wilton Leaf Green Icing Color, as desired
- 1 package (14 oz.) Wilton White Candy Melts, melted

- Crushed peppermint candies, Christmas Sprinkles or Nonpareils, as desired

INSTRUCTIONS

In medium bowl, combine flour, salt and baking powder. In large bowl, beat butter and sugar with electric mixer until light and creamy. Add eggs, vanilla and peppermint candy flavoring; mix well. Add flour mixture, one cup at a time, mixing well after each addition.

Divide dough into thirds. Return ⅓ dough to mixer bowl; beat in red icing color. Roll and shape dough between parchment paper to a 6 x 8 in. disk. Return ⅓ of dough to mixer bowl; mix in green icing color. Roll and shape green dough between parchment paper to a 6 x 8 in. disk. Roll and shape untinted dough between parchment paper to a 6 x 8 in. disk. Chill all dough disks at least 1 hour.

Preheat oven to 350°F. Line cookie sheet with parchment paper. Peel parchment from dough pieces. Stack green and red dough disks aligning them as evenly as possible; gently press pieces together. Add untinted dough rectangle to stack. Gently roll with rolling pin to seal layers; trim uneven edges with sharp knife. Cut dough lengthwise into three 2 in. wide slices; cut each column crosswise into ⅓ in. thick pieces. Arrange 2 in. apart on prepared cookie sheets. Chill ½ hour.

Bake 12-14 minutes or until bottoms are light golden brown. Remove cookies to cooling grids; cool completely.

Dip cooled cookies into melted Candy Melts; sprinkle with crushed candy or sprinkles. Set on parchment-lined cookie pans; chill until candy is set. Store in airtight container.

Makes about 6 dozen cookies.

Potato Chip Cookies

INGREDIENTS

1 pound (4 sticks) unsalted butter, softened
1 cup granulated sugar
1 teaspoon Wilton Pure Vanilla Extract
1½ cups crushed potato chips
3½ cups sifted all-purpose flour
2 packages (14 oz. ea.) Wilton Dark Cocoa Candy Melts (optional)
Additional potato chips, crushed (optional)

INSTRUCTIONS

Preheat oven to 350°F. Line cookie sheets with parchment paper.

In large bowl, beat butter, sugar and vanilla with electric mixer until light and fluffy. Add potato chips; mix until combined. Add flour; stir until just combined. Scoop dough to form 1 in. balls; place 2 in. apart on prepared cookie sheet. Flatten to 1¼ in. thick.

Bake 12-14 minutes or until edges are golden brown. Remove cookies to wire rack; cool completely. If desired, partially dip cookies into melted candy, allowing excess to drip off; sprinkle with crushed potato chips. Allow to set on parchment paper.

Makes about 6 dozen cookies.

RECIPE CONTRIBUTED BY
DORIS BOHLIG, Consumer Affairs Coordinator

"Each year in our subdivision, someone hosts a cookie exchange. I usually bring my potato chip cookies because they are easy to make. One year, I wanted to get more creative and brought a different cookie. Everyone complained and begged for my potato chip cookies."

WILTON
Family Favorite
Cookie Contest
WINNER

Cocoa-Pecan Meringue Cookies

INGREDIENTS

4 cups confectioners' sugar (about 1 lb.)
3 cups pecan halves
⅓ cup unsweetened cocoa powder
6 large egg whites, at room temperature
Wilton Dark Cocoa Candy Melts, melted or Chocolate Ready-To-Use Decorator Icing (optional)

INSTRUCTIONS

Preheat oven to 400°F. Line cookie sheets with parchment paper.

In bowl of food processor, combine confectioners' sugar and pecans; process until nuts are ground to a fine powder, about 2 minutes. Add cocoa; pulse to combine.

In large bowl, beat egg whites with electric mixer until stiff but not dry. Gently fold sugar mixture into eggs, forming a thick batter. Using decorating bag fitted with tip 12, pipe batter onto prepared sheets in walnut-sized mounds, spacing about 1 in. apart (cookies will spread slightly).

Bake 8-10 minutes or until tops appear dry and edges are crisp. Cool completely. If desired, spread bottom of half of the cooled cookies with melted candy or chocolate icing; top with a second cookie to form sandwiches.

Makes about 5 dozen single cookies.

Candy Cane Cookies

INGREDIENTS
1 cup (2 sticks) butter, softened
1 cup granulated sugar
1 egg
1½ teaspoons Wilton Pure Vanilla Extract
½ teaspoon Wilton No-Color Almond Extract
3 cups all-purpose flour
Wilton No-Taste Red Icing Color
Wilton White Sparkling Sugar

INSTRUCTIONS
Preheat oven to 375°F.

In large bowl, beat butter and sugar with mixer until light and fluffy. Beat in egg and extracts. Add flour, 1 cup at a time to butter mixture, mixing well after each addition. If dough becomes too stiff, add water, a teaspoon at a time. Do not chill dough.

Divide dough into 2 balls. Tint one ball of dough red with icing color. Pinch off a 1 in. ball of each color dough. On flat surface, roll ball into 3 in. long strips. Place red and white strips side-by-side; roll them together until the two colors have wrapped around one another and are twisted together. Curve the strip at the top to the shape of a candy cane and place on ungreased cookie sheet; sprinkle with Sparkling Sugar and gently press into dough.

Bake 8-10 minutes or until cookies are lightly browned. Cool on sheet 2 minutes; remove to cooling grid and cool completely.

Makes about 2 dozen cookies.

Holiday Meringue Stars

INGREDIENTS
4 egg whites, at room temperature
¼ teaspoon salt
¼ teaspoon cider vinegar
½ teaspoon Wilton Clear Vanilla Extract
1⅓ cups granulated sugar
2 tablespoons Wilton Christmas Nonpareils + additional
    for topping
1 cup Wilton Dark Cocoa Candy Melts, melted (optional)

INSTRUCTIONS
Preheat oven to 250°F. Line two large cookie sheets with parchment paper.

In large bowl, beat egg whites with electric mixer until frothy. Add salt, vinegar and vanilla; beat at medium-high speed until soft peaks form. Gradually add sugar, one tablespoon at a time, beating on high speed until sugar is nearly dissolved and stiff peaks form. Gently fold in 2 tablespoons nonpareils.

Place mixture in decorating bag fitted with tip 1M; pipe meringue stars 1 in. apart onto prepared sheets. Sprinkle with remaining nonpareils. Place both sheets in oven on separate racks.

Bake 45 minutes. Turn off oven; let meringues dry in oven with door closed for 2 hours. Transfer meringues to cooling grids; cool completely.

If desired, dip bottoms of cooled meringues into melted candy, allowing excess to drip off. Place meringues onto parchment paper; allow to set. Store in airtight containers.

Makes about 6 dozen cookies.

Chocolate Chip Cookies

INGREDIENTS
2 cups all-purpose flour
1 teaspoon baking powder
1 teaspoon baking soda
¾ teaspoon ground cinnamon
½ teaspoon salt
1 cup (2 sticks) butter or margarine, softened
1 cup firmly-packed brown sugar
1 cup granulated sugar
2 eggs
2 teaspoons Wilton Pure Vanilla Extract
1½ cups semi-sweet chocolate chips
½ cup chopped walnuts (optional)

INSTRUCTIONS
Preheat oven to 350°F.

In medium bowl, combine flour, baking powder, baking soda, cinnamon and salt; set aside. In large bowl, beat butter and sugars with electric mixer until light and fluffy. Add eggs and vanilla; mix well. Add flour mixture; mix well. Stir in chocolate chips and, if desired, nuts. Drop by tablespoonfuls onto cookie sheet.

Bake 9-10 minutes or until edges are golden brown. Cool on pan on cooling grid 5 minutes; remove from cookie sheet and cool completely.

To decorate (optional):
Line cookie sheet with parchment paper. Place 1 package (14 oz.) Wilton Light Cocoa Candy Melts in Chocolate Pro Chocolate Melting Pot or microwavable bowl; melt following package instructions. Dip cooled cookies into melted candy; place on lined cookie sheet and allow to set. Using melted red, green and white Candy Melts in separate parchment bags, drizzle over dipped cookies.

Makes about 4 dozen cookies.

Thumbprint Cookies

INGREDIENTS
1 cup all-purpose flour
½ cup finely chopped walnuts
¼ teaspoon salt
½ cup (1 stick) butter, softened
¼ cup firmly-packed brown sugar
1 egg
½ teaspoon Wilton Clear Vanilla Extract
Wilton Candy Melts, bite-size chocolate candy, favorite jam
    or jelly, walnut or pecan pieces

INSTRUCTIONS
Preheat oven to 350°F.

In medium bowl, combine flour, walnuts and salt. In large bowl, beat butter and sugar with electric mixer until light and fluffy. Add egg and vanilla; mix well. Gradually add flour mixture; mix well. Shape dough into 1 in. balls. Place on cookie sheet and make indentation in ball with finger.

Bake 12-15 minutes or until edges are golden brown. Remove cookies from cookie sheet to cooling grid; immediately top with candy, jam or nut. Cool completely. Drizzle cookies with melted candy.

Makes about 2 dozen cookies.

Melting Moments

INGREDIENTS

Cookies:

1 cup (2 sticks) butter, softened

½ cup confectioners' sugar

¾ cup cornstarch

1 cup all-purpose flour

Icing:

3 ounces cream cheese, softened

1 cup confectioners' sugar

½ teaspoon Wilton Clear Vanilla Extract

Wilton Kelly Green Icing Color

Wilton Christmas Nonpareils

INSTRUCTIONS

In large bowl, beat butter and sugar with electric mixer until light and fluffy. Add cornstarch and flour; mix until well blended. Chill dough overnight.

Preheat oven to 350°F.

Scoop or roll 1 in. balls of cookie dough; arrange on cookie sheet 2 in. apart. Bake 10-12 minutes or until edges just begin to brown (Do not overbake.) Remove to cooling grids; cool completely.

For icing, beat cream cheese, confectioners' sugar and vanilla in large bowl with electric mixer until light and fluffy. Add icing color to desired shade. Spread over cookies; sprinkle with nonpareils. If desired, marble 2 shades of green icing, then sprinkle with nonpareils.

Makes about 3 dozen cookies.

RECIPE CONTRIBUTED BY
JULIE SOBOTTA, Product Designer

"These actually melt in your mouth and are never around very long. Children always enjoy them and they are easy to eat for toddlers."

Linzer Sandwich Cookies

INGREDIENTS

2 cups all-purpose flour

⅔ cup finely ground almonds (about 2 oz.)

¼ teaspoon ground cinnamon

¼ teaspoon salt

1 cup (2 sticks) butter, softened

⅔ cup granulated sugar

1 egg

½ teaspoon Wilton Pure Vanilla Extract

½ cup seedless raspberry jam

Confectioners' sugar (optional)

INSTRUCTIONS

In small bowl, combine flour, almonds, cinnamon and salt; set aside. In large bowl, beat butter and sugar with electric mixer until light and fluffy. Add egg and vanilla; mix well. Add flour mixture; mix only until combined. Form dough into 2 disks, about 1 in. thick; wrap in plastic wrap. Chill 2 hours or until firm enough to roll.

Preheat oven to 350°F. Line cookie sheet with parchment paper.

On floured surface, roll out dough ⅛ in. thick (keep remaining dough in refrigerator until ready to roll). Using Wilton Linzer Cutter, cut half of the dough with round cutter and place on prepared pan. Cut remaining dough with round cutter with insert; transfer to second baking sheet. Form scraps into a disk, chill at least 30 minutes and reroll.

Bake 10-12 minutes or until light golden brown. Cool on cookie sheet 2 minutes; remove to cooling grid and cool completely. Spread whole cookies with jam; top with cookies with cut-outs. Gently press together. If desired, lightly dust with confectioners' sugar.

Makes about 20 sandwich cookies.

Heavenly Shortbread

INGREDIENTS

2 cups all-purpose flour

⅛ teaspoon salt

1 cup (2 sticks) butter, softened

⅔ cup granulated sugar

1 egg yolk

2 teaspoons Wilton Pure Vanilla Extract

1 egg

2 tablespoons heavy whipping cream

Wilton White Sparkling Sugar

INSTRUCTIONS

In small bowl, combine flour and salt; set aside. In large bowl, beat butter until light and fluffy; gradually add sugar, beating well. Add egg yolk and vanilla; mix well. Slowly add flour mixture, beating on low speed until incorporated. Increase speed to medium and beat 2 minutes. Form dough into 3 disks, about 1 in. thick; wrap in plastic wrap. Chill 1 hour or until firm enough to roll.

Preheat oven to 350°F. Line cookie sheets with parchment paper.

On floured surface, roll out dough ¼ in. thick (keep remaining dough in refrigerator until ready to roll). Cut with star cutter; place on prepared cookie sheets. Place cookies in freezer for 15 minutes before baking. Form scraps into a disk, chill at least 30 minutes and reroll.

In small bowl, whisk together egg and cream. Remove cookies from freezer and brush lightly with egg mixture. Sprinkle with Sparkling Sugar. Bake 10-12 minutes or until light golden brown. Remove to cooling grid and cool completely.

Makes about 3 dozen cookies.

RECIPE CONTRIBUTED BY
LORI ELLIS, Trainer, Educational Marketing

"This is my all-time favorite cookie! In 2004, it was a finalist in the Fort Worth Star-Telegram's Christmas Cookie Contest—my 1 minute of fame. The egg/whipping cream finish makes the most beautiful crispy top on the cookies."

WILTON Family Favorite Cookie Contest WINNER

Almond Snowballs

INGREDIENTS

1 pound (4 sticks) unsalted butter, softened
1 cup granulated sugar, divided
1 teaspoon Wilton Pure Vanilla Extract
3½ cups all-purpose flour
2 cups (about 8 oz.) ground almonds
Confectioners' sugar

INSTRUCTIONS

Preheat oven to 325°F. Line cookie sheets with parchment paper.

In large bowl, beat butter and granulated sugar with electric mixer until light and fluffy. Add vanilla and mix well. Add flour and almonds; mix with electric mixer on low speed until dough forms. Roll dough into 1 in. balls; place 1 in. apart on cookie sheets.

Bake 20-25 minutes or until bottoms are golden brown. Remove to cooling grid; cool 5 minutes. Roll warm cookies in confectioners' sugar; cool completely.

Makes about 8 dozen cookies.

RECIPE CONTRIBUTED BY
KATHY RYAN, Product Data Specialist

"A rule in our house growing up was that no one could have a cookie until Christmas Eve. They were well-protected on top of the hutch—you needed a chair to even try to reach the tins. This is an extremely easy recipe with few ingredients. You can easily halve the recipe, but the full batch works great for a cookie exchange."

Nana's Knots

INGREDIENTS

Cookies

6 cups all-purpose flour
2 tablespoons baking powder
½ teaspoon salt
6 eggs
1½ cups granulated sugar
1 teaspoon Wilton Clear Vanilla Extract
1 teaspoon Wilton No-Color Almond Extract
¾ cup milk
1 cup (2 sticks) butter, melted and cooled

Icing

4 cups confectioners' sugar (about 1 pound)
7-8 tablespoons milk
½ teaspoon Wilton No-Color Almond Extract
2 jars (10 oz. ea.) maraschino cherries, drained and patted dry
Green spearmint leaves, cut horizontally in thirds (dip cut sides in granulated sugar)

INSTRUCTIONS

Preheat oven to 350°F. Line cookie sheets with parchment paper.

In medium bowl, combine flour, baking powder and salt. In large bowl, beat eggs, sugar and extracts. Add milk and melted butter; mix well. Add flour mixture; mix until soft, slightly elastic dough forms. Dough will be slightly sticky. Using floured hands, form dough into 1 in. balls; roll balls into ½ in. thick logs. Curl logs into snail shapes, tucking end under; place on prepared cookie sheets.

Bake 8-10 minutes or until just beginning to brown on bottoms (Do not overbake). Cool completely on cooling grids.

In medium bowl, combine confectioners' sugar and milk, 1 tablespoon at a time; mix until smooth. Dip cooled cookies in icing, coating completely. Allow icing to set. Cut cherries in half; place one cherry half onto center of each cookie; add spearmint leaf.

Makes about 10 dozen cookies.

RECIPE CONTRIBUTED BY
ANGELA THAYER, Food & Regulatory Specialist

"My husband's great grandmother came over to the U.S. from Italy. She brought with her all of the Italian cooking traditions, including this recipe. Now that Nana is gone my mother-in-law and I have continued the tradition of making these cookies every Christmas. We get to reminisce about Nana's cooking and how loving she was."

Hanseaten Cookies

INGREDIENTS

4 cups sifted all-purpose flour
½ teaspoon baking powder
1 cup (2 sticks) plus 2 tablespoons
   butter, softened
1¼ cups granulated sugar
2 eggs
1 teaspoon Wilton Pure Vanilla
   Extract
1 teaspoon rum extract
½ cup seedless raspberry jam
Wilton Red and White Cookie Icing
Wilton Green and Red Tube Icing

INSTRUCTIONS

In medium bowl, combine flour and baking powder. In large bowl, beat butter and sugar with electric mixer until light and fluffy. Add eggs and extracts; mix well. Add flour mixture; beat only until incorporated. Form dough into 2 disks, about 1 in. thick; wrap in plastic wrap. Refrigerate 2 hours or until firm enough to roll.

Preheat oven to 350°F. Line cookie sheets with parchment paper.

On floured surface, roll out dough ⅛ in. thick (keep remaining dough in refrigerator until ready to roll). Cut with 3 in. round cutter; place on prepared sheet. Form scraps into a disk; chill at least 30 minutes and reroll.

Bake 10-12 minutes or until light golden brown. Remove to cooling grid; cool completely. Spread the bottom of half the cookies with about 1 teaspoon jam. Top with remaining cookies; gently press together.

To decorate, outline with red Cookie Icing, then flood in half of the cookie; allow to set. Use white Cookie Icing to outline and flood remaining half of the cookie. Set completely. Pipe 2 tip 349 holly leaves with green icing; add red tip 3 berries.

Makes about 2 dozen sandwich cookies.

RECIPE CONTRIBUTED BY
ROBIN MUELLER, Senior Field Manager, Educational Marketing

"This cookie has become a family Christmas tradition. It represents our homeland of Germany and the flag of the Hanseatic League, formed around the year 1240 to protect sea ports. The family originally iced them ½ white and ½ red, but we've added our Americanized touch with sprigs of holly berry."

Grandma's Cookies

INGREDIENTS

6 cups all-purpose flour
2 tablespoons baking powder
½ teaspoon salt
1 cup (2 sticks) butter, softened
1½ cups granulated sugar
2 teaspoons anise extract
   (not anise oil)
6 eggs

Icing
4 cups confectioners' sugar
   (about 1 lb.)
7-8 tablespoons warm milk
1 teaspoon anise extract

Wilton White Sparkling Sugar

INSTRUCTIONS

Preheat oven to 350°F. Line cookie sheet with parchment paper.

In medium bowl, combine flour, baking powder and salt. In large bowl, beat butter and granulated sugar until light and fluffy. Add extract and eggs, one at a time, blending well after each. Add flour mixture; mix until soft, slightly elastic dough forms. Using floured hands, form dough into 5 in. long x ½ in. thick logs. Shape into "S" shape; place onto prepared cookie sheets.

Bake 10-12 minutes or until just beginning to brown on bottoms (do not overbake). Remove to cooling grid and cool completely.

In medium bowl, combine confectioners' sugar and milk, 1 tablespoon at a time, until smooth. Dip cooled cookies in icing, coating completely; place on cooling grid set over parchment paper and allow icing to set. Pipe tip 4 confectioners' sugar icing outline along "S"; sprinkle with Sparkling Sugar. Allow to dry.

Makes about 5 dozen cookies.

RECIPE CONTRIBUTED BY
CARMELLA MARKETT, Inside Sales Associate

"My grandmother was from Italy and she made excellent Italian cookies. There were no recipes in those days—everything was measured with your hand. One day, I spent the afternoon with her; as she measured the ingredients with her hands, I took them and put them into standard measuring tools."

Classic Spritz Cookies

INGREDIENTS

3½ cups all-purpose flour
1 teaspoon baking powder
1½ cups (3 sticks) butter, softened
1 cup granulated sugar
1 egg
2 tablespoons milk
1 teaspoon Wilton Pure Vanilla Extract
½ teaspoon Wilton No-Color Almond Extract

INSTRUCTIONS

Preheat oven to 350°F.

In medium bowl, combine flour and baking powder. In large bowl, beat butter and sugar with electric mixer until light and fluffy. Add egg, milk and extracts. Add flour mixture; mix well. Fill cookie press with dough and fit with desired disks; press cookies onto ungreased cookie sheet.

Bake 10-12 minutes or until edges are light golden brown. Cool 2 minutes on cookie sheet; remove to cooling grid and cool completely.

Makes 7-8 dozen cookies

ORANGE SPRITZ COOKIES

Substitute orange juice for milk in basic recipe. Omit almond extract. Add 2 tablespoons grated orange zest and, if desired, ¼ cup finely chopped pecans (optional).

GINGERBREAD SPRITZ COOKIES

Substitute firmly-packed dark brown sugar for granulated sugar in basic recipe. Omit extracts. Add ½ teaspoon each ground allspice, ground cloves, ground cinnamon and ground ginger.

POTATO CHIP SPRITZ COOKIES

Reduce flour in basic recipe to 2⅔ cups; combine with 1½ cups finely crushed potato chips. Reduce granulated sugar to ¾ cup. Omit almond extract.

CREAM CHEESE SPRITZ COOKIES

Substitute 6 ounces (¾ of an 8-oz. package) cream cheese, softened, for ½ cup (1 stick) butter in basic recipe. Increase granulated sugar to 1¼ cups. Omit almond extract. Add 2 teaspoons lemon zest.

Gingerbread Cookies

INGREDIENTS

3 cups all-purpose flour
½ teaspoon baking soda
½ teaspoon salt
1 teaspoon ground ginger
1 teaspoon ground cinnamon
½ teaspoon ground nutmeg
½ teaspoon ground cloves
½ cup solid vegetable shortening
½ cup granulated sugar
¾ cup molasses
1 egg, beaten

INSTRUCTIONS

Preheat oven to 375°F.

In large bowl, combine flour, baking soda, salt and spices. In large saucepan, melt shortening; cool slightly. Stir in sugar, molasses and egg; mix well. Add 2 cups flour mixture; mix well.

Turn mixture onto lightly floured surface. Knead in remaining flour mixture by hand. Add additional flour, if necessary, to make firm dough. Roll out on a lightly floured surface, ⅛ to ¼ in. thick.

Bake on ungreased cookie sheet until lightly browned on edges, about 10-15 minutes for large sized cookies, 6-10 minutes for small to medium sized cookies. Cool on cookie sheet placed on cooling grid 3 minutes; remove from cookie sheet and cool completely.

Makes about 2 dozen cookies.

Substitute ¾ cup light corn syrup for molasses to make Blonde Gingerbread.

Roll-Out Cookies

INGREDIENTS
- 2¾ cups all-purpose flour
- 2 teaspoons baking powder
- 1 teaspoon salt
- 1 cup (2 sticks) unsalted butter, softened
- 1½ cups granulated sugar
- 1 egg
- 1½ teaspoons Wilton Pure Vanilla Extract
- ½ teaspoon Wilton No-Color Almond Extract

INSTRUCTIONS
Preheat oven to 400°F.

In medium bowl, combine flour, baking powder and salt. In large bowl, beat butter and sugar until light and fluffy. Beat in egg and extracts. Add flour mixture to butter mixture, 1 cup at a time, mixing after each addition. Do not chill dough.

Divide dough into 2 balls. On a floured surface, roll each ball into a circle approximately 12 in. diameter and ⅛ in. thick. Dip cookie cutter in flour before each use.

Bake cookies on ungreased cookie sheet 6-7 minutes or until cookies are lightly browned.

Makes about 3 dozen 3 in. cookies.

LEMON CUT-OUTS
Substitute ½ teaspoon lemon extract for almond extract. Stir 3 tablespoons lemon zest (about 3 lemons) into cookie dough with flour mixture.

PEPPERMINT CUT-OUTS
Add ⅓ cup peppermint crunch sprinkles or finely crushed peppermint candies to cookie dough with flour mixture.

COCONUT CUT-OUTS
Add 1 cup toasted shredded coconut, finely chopped, to cookie dough with flour mixture.

CARROT CUT-OUTS
Add ¾ teaspoon ground cinnamon, ¼ teaspoon ground nutmeg, and ¼ teaspoon ground cloves to flour mixture. Add 1¼ cups finely grated carrots and, if desired, ¼ cup finely chopped walnuts to cookie dough with flour mixture.

CHOCOLATE ORANGE CUT-OUTS
Add 3 squares (3 oz.) unsweetened chocolate, melted and cooled, to butter mixture before adding flour mixture. Stir 2 tablespoons grated orange zest into cookie dough with flour mixture.

Royal Icing

INGREDIENTS
- 3 tablespoons Wilton Meringue Powder
- 4 cups sifted confectioners' sugar (about 1 pound)
- 6 tablespoons water*

INSTRUCTIONS
Beat all ingredients with electric mixer at low speed for 7-10 minutes (10-12 minutes at high speed for portable mixer) until icing forms peaks. Makes about 3 cups.

*When using large countertop mixer or for stiffer icing, use 1 tablespoon less water.

Thinned Royal Icing: To thin for pouring, add 1 tablespoon water per cup of royal icing. Use grease-free spoon or spatula to stir slowly. Add ½ teaspoon water at a time until you reach proper consistency.

Color Flow Icing
(full-strength for outlining)

INGREDIENTS
- ¼ cup + 1 teaspoon water
- 4 cups sifted confectioners' sugar (about 1 pound)
- 2 tablespoons Color Flow Mix

INSTRUCTIONS
With electric mixer, using grease-free utensils, blend all ingredients on low speed for 5 minutes. If using hand mixer, use high speed. Color flow icing "crusts" quickly, so keep bowl covered with a damp cloth while using. Stir in desired icing color. Makes about 2 cups.

Thinned Color Flow: To fill an outlined area, the recipe above must be thinned with ⅛ teaspoon of water per ¼ cup of icing (just a few drops at a time as you near proper consistency). Use grease-free spoon or spatula to stir slowly. Color flow is ready for filling in outlines when a small amount dropped into the mixture takes a count of 10 to disappear.

Note: Color flow designs take a long time to dry, so plan to do your color flow piece at least 1 or 2 days in advance.

Sugar Cookies (for non-stick pans)

INGREDIENTS
- 1 cup (2 sticks) butter, softened
- 1½ cups granulated sugar
- 1 egg
- 1½ teaspoons Wilton Pure Vanilla Extract
- ½ teaspoon Wilton No-Color Almond Extract (optional)
- 2¾ cups all-purpose flour
- 1 teaspoon salt

INSTRUCTIONS
Preheat oven to 350°F. Lightly spray pan cavities with vegetable pan spray.

In large bowl, use electric mixer at medium speed to beat butter and sugar until well blended. Beat in egg and extracts; blend well. Combine flour and salt; add to butter mixture and beat until well blended.

Press dough into cavities, filling ⅔ full. Bake 9-10 minutes or until light brown around edges. Cool in pan 5 minutes. Turn pan over; lightly tap to remove cookies. Cool completely on cooling grid.

Makes about 3 dozen cookies.

Cookie Products

Having lots of choices is what a cookie exchange is all about. After you shop the wide selection of Wilton cookie products here, you'll be ready to bake and decorate just about any style of holiday cookie! You'll find a multitude of jolly cutter shapes, toppings in a rainbow of colors, pans and tools designed for better baking results and presentation products ready to dress your treats in harmony with the holidays. Look for even more cookie making and decorating products at www.wilton.com.

Cookie Presses

Wilton has the best selection of feature-packed presses anywhere! From our Comfort Grip Press, designed for easy handling and filling, to our powerful cordless Cookie Master Plus, spritz cookie-making has never been easier!

Making traditional spritz cookies has never been so easy! Cookie Pro Ultra II is designed to be the easiest to fill, most comfortable press you've ever used. With 12 terrific shapes, plus 4 fun mini cookie designs, your holiday cookie baskets will be more festive than ever! Includes complete instructions and delicious recipes. Set/17 **2104-4018**

Twelve Disks in Festive Shapes

Plus 4 BONUS Disks For Mini Cookies!

COOKIE MASTER™ *Plus*
Cordless Cookie Press

Our cordless cookie press is so powerful and easy to operate, you'll use it all year to create cookies, appetizers, desserts and more. Exclusive patented reverse action means there's no need to take press apart for refilling. Ergonomic design is shaped to fit in your hand for excellent comfort.

Includes 12 aluminum disks in classic and seasonal shapes, 4 accent tips for decorating and filling and 2 bonus recipe booklets—sweet and savory. Uses 4 AA batteries, not included. Patent Nos. D484,755, and 6,701,828. Set/19 **2104-4008**

12 Disk Designs

4 Accent Tips

COMFORT GRIP™
Cookie Press

Experience a classic press that is truly comfortable. Its ergonomic handle feels great in your hand and the easy-squeeze action releases perfectly shaped dough. Clear barrel takes the guesswork out of refilling. Fluted bottom raises press off the cookie sheet for better-defined shapes. Includes 12 cookie disks in a variety of shapes and our classic spritz recipe. Set/13 **2104-4011**

12 Disk Designs

Cookie Cutters

Wilton has the cutter shapes and styles you need to set your cookies apart! Check out our variety—from cutter collections and theme sets that cover any occasion to extra-deep Comfort-Grip Cutters in favorite holiday shapes, Wilton is your most complete source for cookie fun!

Round
2310-608

Candy Cane
2310-644

Santa Hat
2310-640

Christmas Tree
2310-604

Snowflake
2310-592

Gingerbread Boy
2310-602

Mitten
2310-639

Snowman
2310-634

Star
2310-631

Comfort-Grip Cutters
These easy-grip cutters with extra-deep sides are perfect for cutting so many favorite foods into spectacular shapes. The cushion grip gives you comfortable control even when cutting thick desserts. Recipe included. Stainless steel sides, 4.5 x 4.5 x 1.5 in. deep.

Christmas Push-N-Print Cutter Set
Serve cookies that make a great impression—use Push-N-Print Cutters to emboss a fun design before baking! It's so easy! Load one of the 3 imprint disks in the cutter, cut the cookie, then press the plunger with disk still in place to imprint the design. Bake, cool and serve a treat that's perfect for celebrations and cookie gift baskets. Great for embossed fondant decorations too! Disks are 2.9 in. diameter. Plastic. Recipe included. Set/4 **2308-4003**

7 Pc. Linzer Cut Outs Cookie Cutter Set
Make European-inspired jam-filled cookies for a fun holiday treat. Fluted round cookie cutter has 6 interchangeable center shapes: star, heart, flower, triangle, diamond and circle that let the filling show through. Cookies approx. 3 in. Metal. Recipe included. Set/7 **2308-3800**

18 Pc. Holiday Cutter Set
Snowflake, holly leaf, gingerbread girl, star, sleigh, tree, stocking, snowman, reindeer, ornament, candy cane, Santa hat, angel, gingerbread boy, mitten, bell, gift and wreath. Metal. Each approx. 3 in. Set/18 **2308-1132**

9 Pc. Holiday Cutter Set
Candy cane, gingerbread girl, stocking, angel, star, bell, snowman, tree and gingerbread boy, each approx. 3 to 3.75 in. Colored aluminum. Set/9 **2308-2500**

3 Pc. Holiday Cutter Set
Set of 3 includes present, star and ornament, each approx. 2.5 to 3.25 in. Coated metal. Set/3 **2308-1118**

3 Pc. Winter Cookie Cutter Set
Stocking, mitten and dove, each approx. 2.5 to 3.25 in. Coated metal. Recipe included. Set/3 **2308-1101**

3 Pc. Holiday Cutter Set
Santa, reindeer and present, each approx. 2.75 to 3.25 in. Coated metal. Recipe included. Set/3 **2308-1104**

3 Pc. Snowflake Cookie Cutter Set
Stylized, wavy and straight-edge snowflakes, each approx. 3.25 in. Coated metal. Recipe included. Set/3 **2308-1106**

3 Pc. Christmas Trees Cookie Cutter Set
Triangle tree, star-top tree and classic fir, each approx. 3 in. Coated metal. Recipe included. Set/3 **2308-1103**

3 Pc. Christmas Cutter Set
Set of 3 includes snowflake, gingerbread boy and tree, each approx. 3 to 3.75 in. Coated metal. Set/3 **2308-1266**

3 Pc. Gingerbread Cutter Set
Gingerbread boy, girl and house, each approx. 3 to 3.5 in. Coated metal. Recipe included. Set/3 **2308-1102**

4 Pc. Grippy Cutter Set
Safe, easy cutting, with a comfortable grip and deep plastic sides. Four shapes include stocking, tree, star and gingerbread boy, each approx. 3.5 in. Set/4 **2311-260**

101 Cookie Cutters Set
Make cookies featuring popular holiday and theme shapes. Average cutter size approx. 3.5 x 3.5 in. Recipe included. Plastic. Set/101 **2304-1050**

6 Pc. Holiday Mini Cutter Set
Gingerbread boy, tree, gingerbread girl, dove, mitten and stocking, each approx. 1.75 in. Metal. Recipe included. Set/6 **2308-1108**

6 Pc. Holiday Mini Cutter Set
3 stars, 3 snowflakes, each approx. 1.5 in. Metal. Recipe included. Set/6 **2308-1110**

6 Pc. Nesting Hearts Cutter Set
Great for cookies, imprinting patterns in icing, cutting bread shapes and more. Plastic in sizes from 2.25 to 4.2 in. Set/6 **2304-115**

Snowflakes 2308-1244   **Gingerbread Boys 2308-1239**

4 Pc. Nesting Cutter Sets
Bake your favorite holiday shapes in four fun sizes! Quality metal cuts neatly and is easy to handle. Sizes from 5 to 2.5 in. Set/4

6 Pc. Nesting Stars Cutter Set
Plastic. 1.6 to 4.6 in. Set/6 **2304-704**

6 Pc. Holiday Mini Cutter Set
Reindeer, Santa, 3 ornaments, present, each approx. 1.5 to 2 in. Metal. Recipe included. Set/6 **2308-1109**

12 Pc. Holiday Mini Cutter Set
Star, angel, gingerbread girl, stocking, candy cane, ornament, teddy bear, bell, holly leaf, tree, gingerbread boy and sleigh. Metal. Each approx. 1.5 in. Set/12 **2308-1250**

Round 417-432   **Heart 417-434**

3 Pc. Cut-Outs Sets
With Cut-Outs, it's easy to make fun cookies or fondant shapes. Just roll out, press down with Cut-Out and lift away. Remove shapes with a small spatula. Stainless steel shapes range from .6 in. to 2.5 in.

Christmas Cupcake and Cookie Stencils
Turn plain treats into holiday visions. Just place 1 of the 8 fun designs over your iced treat, then sprinkle with Wilton Cake Sparkles or Colored Sugars (p. 92) or use FoodWriter Edible Ink Markers or Color Mist Food Color Spray. 8 designs. **417-510**

Christmas Cookie Tree Cutter Kit
Create a beautiful Yule tree as a perfect holiday centerpiece. . . it's easy and fun! Just bake, stack and decorate. Kit includes 10 plastic star cookie cutters in graduated sizes, 3 disposable decorating bags, round decorating tip, cookie and icing recipes, baking and decorating instructions for 4 great designs. Tree measures approx. 8 x 11 in. high when assembled. **2104-1555**

Cookie Treat Sticks
For fun cookie pops. 6 in. Pk./20 **1912-9319**

8 in. Pk./20 **1912-9318**

13 Pc. Cookie Decorating Set
Be ready for your cookie exchange with the most festive cookies of the season! Decorating is fast and fun with the essential tips, bags and stencils included. Set contains 5 decorating tips, 6 disposable decorating bags, 2-pc. stencil set and complete instruction sheet. Set/13 **2104-2538**

Tools & Preparation Products

A complete cookie collection, designed for better mixing and baking results.

Roll & Cut Mat
For precise measuring, rolling and cutting of fondant or dough. Pre-marked circles for exact sizing. Square grid helps you cut precise strips. Non-stick surface for easy release. 20 in. square with circles from 3 in. to 19 in. diam.
409-412

Pastry Mat
Non-stick mat with pre-marked measurements for easy rolling and precise cutting! Includes circles for pie, tart and pizza crusts from 6 to 16 in. diameter, pre-marked inches and centimeters for exact cutting of lattice strips. Delicious cookie and pie crust recipes are printed on the mat. 18 x 24 in.
409-413

Silicone Baking Mat
Line cookie sheets—protects against burned bottoms and cleans up with ease! Or, use as a pastry mat.
10 x 15 in.
2105-4808

Liquid Measuring Cups
Unique step design lets you read measurements from above. Patent Pending.
2 Cup 2103-334

4 Cup 2103-335

Silicone Spoon Scraper
One tool is all you need for scooping, scraping and mixing. Flexible pointed tip gets into hard-to-reach corners. Patent No. D584,927. 11 in. long.
2103-328

Stainless Steel Cookie Scoops
Scoops uniform portions of dough; spring handle for easy release.
Regular 8 in. long **417-141**
Large 8.5 in. long **417-139**

12 in. Rolling Pin
Easy cleaning and smooth rolling! It's fully-submersible, with non-slip surface and push-button handle release. Barrel measures 11.25 in. Patent Pending.
2103-301

20 in. Fondant Roller
Extra-wide, smooth design, great for rolling out pastry and cookie dough.
1907-1210

Jumbo Cookie Spatula/Lifter
Generously-sized spatula is great for handling multiple or oversized cookies, brownies, pastries and large treat bars. The easy-grip handle helps balance large cookies and desserts. Stainless steel, dishwasher safe.
11 in. long.
570-2018

Holiday Red Cookie Scoop
Scoops and releases approx. 1 tablespoon of dough with ease.
8.25 in. long.
417-320

Scoop-It Measuring Tools
Unique spade shaped design. Snap-on ring gives easy access to each cup or spoon.
Cups
Includes 1 cup, ½ cup, ⅓ cup, ¼ cup. Patent No. D582,297. Set/4
2103-324

Spoons
Includes 1 tablespoon, 1 teaspoon, ½ teaspoon, ¼ teaspoon, ⅛ teaspoon. Patent No. D582,298. Set/5
2103-325

Silicone Stand Mixer Scraper
Angled neck and unique flexible silicone head easily mix dough back into bottom of bowl with mixer attachment in place. Patent No. D587,537. 11 in. long.
2103-329

Silicone Universal Scraper
Flat, flexible end for pans and bowls, small rounded end for jars. Patent No. D586,630. 11 in. long.
2103-327

Tilt-N-Mix 3 Pc. Bowl Set
Bowls tip at an angle without falling over—makes mixing easy!. Includes 1.5, 3 and 5 quart bowls. Set/3
2103-306

Bake Easy! Non-Stick Spray
This convenient non-stick spray helps your baked goods release perfectly. Just a light, even coating does the job. Versatile for all types of baking and cooking. 6 oz.
702-6018

Icing Spatulas
Decorate with more control and less fatigue. The ergonomic handle features a finger pad, which tapers to the flexible stainless steel blade for better control.

Straight
Great for spreading and smoothing fillings, all-around kitchen use.
9 in. **409-6045**
11 in. **409-6046**
15 in. **409-6047**

Angled
Ideal angle for smoothing cake sides and spreading fillings.
9 in. **409-6040**
13 in. **409-6041**
15 in. **409-6042**

Tapered
Easily ices hard-to-reach spots on your cake.
9 in. **409-6057**

Non-Stick Parchment Paper
Use Wilton silicone-treated non-stick parchment to line baking pans and cookie sheets—a non-fat alternative that saves cleanup time. Double roll is 41 square feet, 15 in. wide. Certified Kosher. **415-680**

Sprinkles

Pour on the fun! Great shapes and colors add a dash of excitement to cookies, cakes, cupcakes, ice cream and more. Certified Kosher.

Colored Sugar
Wilton sugar is excellent for filling in brightly colored designs on cakes, cupcakes and cookies. 3.25 oz. bottle. Certified Kosher.

Blue 710-750	**Light Green** 710-752	**Pink** 710-756	**Lavender** 710-758
Orange 710-759	**Dark Green** 710-764	**Red** 710-766	**Yellow** 710-754

Sparkling Sugar
Easy-pour sugars have a coarse texture and brilliant sparkle. 8 oz. bottle. Certified Kosher.

White 710-992	**Red/White** 710-998	**Green/White** 710-997

Cake Sparkles
Edible glitter in .25 oz. bottle. Certified Kosher.

White 703-1290	**Yellow** 703-1272

Pearlized Sugars
Add a shimmering look with these softly-shaded pearlized toppings. Your cakes and cupcakes will shine with new jewel-tone colored sugars and sugar pearls. 5.25 oz. bottle. Certified Kosher.

Gold 710-041	**Silver** 710-042	**White** 710-043	**Sugar Pearls** 710-044	**Red** 710-046	**Sapphire** 710-047	**Green** 710-048

Jumbo Sprinkles
Big bold toppers perfect for cookies, brownies and more. Plastic bottles for convenient pouring and storing. Certified Kosher.

Snowflakes 2.6 oz. bottle. 710-569	**Nonpareils** 4.8 oz. bottle. 710-033	**Confetti** 3.25 oz. bottle. 710-029	**Stars** 3.25 oz. bottle. 710-026

Shaped Sprinkles
Shake up your holiday treats with fun colors and designs. Plastic bottles for convenient pouring and storing. Certified Kosher.

Christmas Confetti 2 oz. bottle. 710-172	**Christmas Nonpareils** 3 oz. bottle. 710-585	**Rainbow Nonpareils** 3 oz. bottle. 710-772	**Snowflake Mix** 2.5 oz. bottle. 710-797	**White Nonpareils** 3 oz. bottle. 710-773	**Cinnamon Drops** 3 oz. bottle. 710-769

6-Mix Assortments
Assorted fun shapes in an easy-pour flip-top bottle. Certified Kosher.

Flowerful Medley
Includes Confetti, Colorful Leaves, Daisies, Pastel Hearts, Wild Flowers, Butterflies. 2.23 oz. total.
710-4122

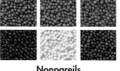

Nonpareils
Includes Pink, Orange, Green, Red, Yellow, Purple. 3 oz. total.
710-4125

Non-Stick Steel & Aluminum Bakeware

Wilton has the quality pans you need for every type of cookie. Even-heating designs provide great baking results year after year.

6 Cavity Gingerbread Village Non-Stick Cookie Pan
Create a captivating Christmas scene with 6 house fronts in a variety of festive shapes. Just press dough in pan, bake and release. 6 cavities, each approx. 3.25 x 4 x .25 in. deep.
2105-8147

12 Cavity Holiday Shapes Non-Stick Cookie Pan
Includes 12 classic shapes! Just press dough in cavities and the great detail bakes right in. 12 cavities, each approx. 2.75 x 2.25 x .25 in. deep.
2105-8122

Air-Insulated Non-Stick Cookie Sheet
Two quality aluminized steel layers sandwich an insulating layer of air for perfect browning without burning. 18 x 14 in.
2105-978

Round Cookie Treat Pan
Just press dough into pan, insert a cookie stick and bake for a fun treat. 6 cavities, each 3.5 x .25 in. deep.
2105-8105

Chrome Cooling Grids
Sturdy design will never rust.
14.5 x 20 in.
2305-129

13 in. Round
2305-130

Non-Stick Pans
Built to bake better, with durable reinforced non-stick coating and heavy-duty warp-resistant steel construction.

Jelly Roll/Cookie Pan
10.5 x 15.5 x 1 in.
2105-967

Oblong Cake Pan
13 x 9 x 2 in.
2105-961

Square Baking Pan
8 x 8 x 2 in.
2105-956

Aluminum Pans
Best for even-heating performance, Wilton aluminum is extra thick for perfectly browned bottoms.

Jelly Roll/Cookie Pan
12 x 18 x 1 in.
2105-4854

Jumbo Cookie Sheet
14 x 20 in.
2105-6213

Pearl Dust

Add rich, lustrous color highlights—just brush onto cookies! .05 oz. bottle. Certified Kosher.

Green 703-215	Yellow 703-213	Gold 703-216
Silver 703-218	White 703-219	Red 703-223

Icing Colors

Easy-mixing colors are great for tinting cookie dough or icings!

Produce deep, rich color with just a small amount using this fast-mixing gel. The Wilton exclusive concentrated gel formula was developed to help decorators achieve the exact shade desired without changing icing consistency. An unmatched color selection makes it easy for you to achieve virtually any shade.

*Note: Large amounts of these colors may affect icing taste. Use No-Taste Red for large areas of red on a cake. When using Black, start with chocolate icing to limit the amount of color needed.

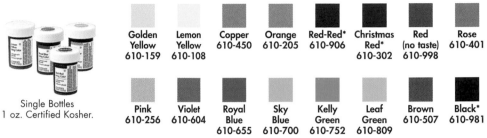

Single Bottles 1 oz. Certified Kosher.

Golden Yellow 610-159	Lemon Yellow 610-108	Copper 610-450	Orange 610-205	Red-Red* 610-906	Christmas Red* 610-302	Red (no taste) 610-998	Rose 610-401
Pink 610-256	Violet 610-604	Royal Blue 610-655	Sky Blue 610-700	Kelly Green 610-752	Leaf Green 610-809	Brown 610-507	Black* 610-981

Icings, Gels & Flavors

Create every colorful effect with our convenient mixes and ready-to-use icings.

Tube Decorating Icing

Can be used with our Coupler Ring Set and any standard size Wilton metal tip. Colors match Wilton Icing Colors above. 4.25 oz. Certified Kosher.

Kelly Green	704-227
Red	704-218
Leaf Green	704-224
White	704-200
Chocolate	704-254

Coupler Ring Set (not shown) Attach Wilton standard size tips onto our tube icings to create any technique. Set/4 **418-47306**

Tube Decorating Gel

Transparent gels are great for writing messages and decorating cakes and cookies. Colors match Wilton Icing Colors above. .75 oz. Certified Kosher.

Leaf Green	704-324
Red	704-318
White	704-302

Meringue Powder

Primary ingredient for royal icing. Stabilizes buttercream, adds body to boiled icing and meringue. Replaces egg whites in many recipes. Resealable top opens for easy measuring. 4 oz. can makes 5 recipes of royal icing; 8 oz. can makes 10 recipes. 16 oz. can makes 20 recipes. Certified Kosher.

4 oz.	702-6007
8 oz.	702-6015
16 oz.	702-6004

Pure Vanilla Extract

The world's finest vanilla is from Madagascar. Unmatched flavor and aroma enhances cookies, cakes, puddings, pie fillings, custards and more. 4 fl. oz. Certified Kosher. **604-2270**

Cookie Icing

Easy to use—just heat and squeeze onto cookies using the convenient cap. Sets smooth in just 45-60 minutes. 10 oz. bottle covers approximately 12 cookies, 3 in. each; 20 oz. bottle covers approx. 24. Certified Kosher.

Green	10 oz.	704-493
Red	10 oz.	704-488
White	10 oz.	704-481
White	20 oz.	704-492

Sparkle Gel

Squeeze on sparkling color effects with our ready-to-use gel. Great for dots, messages and fondant accents. Resealable 3.5 oz. tube. Certified Kosher.

Green	704-111
Red	704-112
Yellow	704-108
White	704-107

Piping Gel

Pipe messages and designs or glaze cookies to hold sprinkles and sugars. Use clear or tint with icing color. 10 oz. Certified Kosher. **704-105**

No-Color Flavors

These delicious flavors won't change your icing color. Essential for making pure white icings and maintaining vibrant colors in all your decorating. Certified Kosher.

Clear Vanilla Extract
2 fl. oz. **604-2237**
8 fl. oz. **604-2269**

Clear Almond Extract
2 fl. oz. **604-2126**

Clear Butter Flavor
2 fl. oz. **604-2040**
8 fl. oz. **604-2067**

Ready-to-Decorate Icing

Anyone can decorate with Wilton Ready-to-Decorate Icing! Our brilliant colors and four decorating tips make it a breeze to add an exciting finishing touch to treats—without mixing or mess. 6.4 oz. Certified Kosher.

Green	710-4401
Red	710-4400
White	710-4402

Color Flow Mix

Create dimensional flow-in designs for your cake. Just add water and confectioners' sugar. 4 oz. can makes ten 1½ cup batches. Certified Kosher. **701-47**

Primary Colors Fondant Multi Pack

Convenient four-pouch assortment perfect for cookie accents. Each 17.6 oz. package contains four 4.4 oz. packs. Certified Kosher. Green, Red, Yellow, Blue **710-445**

Decorating Bags

All decorating bags are not the same! Wilton bags are tested to be the best. They simply feel better in your hand—soft and strong to provide decorating performance you can count on. From pure parchment triangles to our convenient Disposable or premium reusable Featherweight styles, Wilton bags are made to our strict specifications for consistent quality.

Featherweight Decorating Bags

The best quality bags for decorating, with strong resilient seams to help them last for years! Featherweight bags feel soft and comfortable in the hand—the polyester material becomes softer the more the bags are used. Lightweight, strong and flexible, they'll never get stiff. Coated to prevent grease from seeping through. Each batch is tested in the Wilton Test Kitchen to meet our exacting standards. Dishwasher safe. Instructions included; sold singly.

8 in. **404-5087**
10 in. **404-5109**
12 in. **404-5125**
14 in. **404-5140**
16 in. **404-5168**
18 in. **404-5184**

Parchment Triangles

Authentic parchment paper is the professional's choice for convenience and quick bag preparation. Make use-and-toss decorating bags ideal for small amounts of icing or brush striping. Excellent wet strength for candy or a variety of icings. Also great for smoothing iced cakes and transferring patterns. 15 in. Pk./100
2104-1508

Disposable Decorating Bags

Wilton's strict testing standards ensure the highest quality disposable bags you can buy. Our proprietary blend of materials helps Wilton bags feel more comfortable and outperform competitive bags. They can be used with or without a coupler and work great for microwave-melting and piping of Candy Melts. Fits standard tips and couplers. Just use, then toss! Instructions included.

12 in. Pk./12 **2104-358**
12 in. Pk./24 **2104-1358**
16 in. Pk./12 **2104-1357**

Candy

With easy-melting Candy Melts, concentrated candy colors and convenient molds, it's easy to add fun candy accents to your cookies. Candy is great for drizzling, dipping and attaching decorations to cookies!

Candy Melts

Delicious, creamy, easy-to-melt wafers are ideal for all your candy making—molding, dipping or coating. Their delicious taste can be varied by adding our Candy Flavors. Light and Dark Cocoa are made with real cocoa; colors are artificially vanilla flavored unless otherwise noted. 14 oz. bag. Certified Kosher Dairy.

Peanut Butter 1911-481	**Dark Cocoa** 1911-358	**Light Cocoa** 1911-544	**Dark Cocoa Mint** 1911-1920	**Lavender** 1911-403	**Pink** 1911-447
Yellow 1911-463	**Orange** 1911-1631	**Blue** 1911-448	**Red** 1911-499	**Green** 1911-405	**White** 1911-498

Primary Candy Color Set

Concentrated oil-based colors blend easily with Candy Melts. Includes Yellow, Orange, Red and Blue in .25 oz. jars. Certified Kosher. Set/4
1913-1299

Garden Candy Color Set

Create pretty pastel colors! Concentrated oil-based colors blend easily with Candy Melts. Includes Pink, Green, Violet and Black in .25 oz. jars. Certified Kosher. Set/4
1913-1298

Dessert Accents Mold

Finish your signature dessert with flair—top it with a dramatic candy shape using this exciting mold. Swirls, scrolls, zigzags, triangles and leaves add 5-star style. 5 designs, 10 cavities.
2115-2102

Cordial Cups Mold

Mold a candy "glass" for dessert liqueurs, or fill with whipped cream and float in cocoa or coffee. 1 design, 6 cavities.
2115-1535

Lollipop Sticks

Sturdy paper sticks. Not for oven use.
8 in. Pk./25
1912-9320

11¾ in. Pk./20
1912-1212

Brush Set

Fine-bristle brushes in three tip designs (round, square and bevel), help you achieve different painted effects. Set/3
1907-1207

Chocolate Pro Electric Melting Pot

The fast and easy way to melt chocolate and Candy Melts for fun dipped cookies!
- Melting base stays cool to the touch
- Removeable non-stick Melting Pot holds 2½ cups
- Easy-pour spout
- Non-skid feet keep Chocolate Pro steady

120 volts. CUL Listed. **2104-9004**

Winter 2115-1360

Holiday 2115-1359

Cookie Candy Molds

Turn store-bought cookies into candy-coated treats! Use with Wilton Candy Melts to make festively detailed holiday cookies. Just brush melted Candy Melts into color detail areas; let set, then complete molding with more melted candy and your favorite sandwich cookie, 2 in. diameter or less.

Presentation

Protect your treats with winter white boxes and clear bags ready for your favorite colorful trims. Find festive holiday accents to complete the look at www.wilton.com and www.eksuccess.com.

Hexagon Treat Boxes
Self-closing top forms a pretty petal box top. Great for cookies, candy and favors. 4 x 6.25 in. high. White Pk./4 **415-105**

Square Treat Boxes
Create the perfect gift with window boxes. Great for candies, cookies or other treats. Medium boxes include insert for 4 cupcakes. Small includes seals/sticker sheet. White.
Small
4.5 x 4.5 x 1.5 in. Pk./3
415-102

Medium
6.25 x 6.25 x 3 in. Pk./3
415-1215

Candy Treat Boxes
Your tempting cookie gifts show through the front window. Tented design holds pretzels or biscotti upright to protect against breakage. 3 x 2 x 9.5 in. high. White. **1904-2000**

Popcorn Treat Boxes
Classic shape stands up tall to hold cookies and other snacks. 3.75 x 2.25 x 5.25 in. high. White. Pk./4 **1904-1141**

Tent Treat Boxes
Stand-up design with front window will give your homemade treat gift the ideal showcase. 3.25 x 1.6 x 5.75 in. high. White. Pk./3 **1904-1087**

Treat Baskets
Roomy handled basket is ideal for your gifts. Great for muffins, mini loaves and more. 6.5 x 6.5 x 3 in. Pk./2 **415-104**

Large Treat Bags
Ideal size for Treat Baskets filled with cookies or muffins. Great for a cookie platter, pie, scones and more. Includes 3 - 16 x 20 in. bags; 3 - 18 in. ribbons, 3 gift tags. **1912-1143**

Medium Treat Bags
Wrap up bread loaves, smaller bowls and plates of treats. Includes 4 - 10 x 16 in. bags; 4 - 18 in. ribbons, 4 gift tags. **1912-1142**

Clear Party Bags
4 x 9.5 in. Each pack contains 25 bags and 25 ties. Pk./25 **1912-1240**

Fanci-Foil Wrap
Serving side has a non-toxic grease-resistant surface. Continuous roll: 20 in. x 15 ft.
Silver **804-167**

Cake Circles
Corrugated cardboard for strength and stability.
6 in. diameter Pk./10 **2104-64**
8 in. diameter Pk./12 **2104-80**
10 in. diameter Pk./12 **2104-102**
12 in. diameter Pk./8 **2104-129**
14 in. diameter Pk./6 **2104-145**
16 in. diameter Pk./6 **2104-160**

Pre-Baked Gingerbread House Kit
Includes pre-baked gingerbread pieces, icing mix, assorted candies, decorating bag and tip, cardboard base, complete instructions and decorating ideas. House measures 8 x 7 x 6.5 in. high.
2104-1509

Keeping in Touch with Wilton

There's always something new at Wilton! Fun decorating courses that will help your decorating skills soar. Exciting cake designs to challenge you. Great new decorating products to try. Helpful hints to make your decorating more efficient and successful. Here's how you can keep up to date with what's happening at Wilton.

Decorating Classes

Do you want to learn more about cake decorating, with the personal guidance of a Wilton instructor? Wilton has two ways to help you.

The Wilton School of Cake Decorating and Confectionery Art is the home of the world's most popular cake decorating curriculum. For more than 80 years, thousands of students from around the world have learned to decorate cakes using The Wilton Method. In 1929, Dewey McKinley Wilton taught the first small classes in his Chicago home. Today, The Wilton School teaches more people to decorate than any school in the world. As the school has grown, some techniques have been refined and there are more classes to choose from—but the main philosophies of the Wilton Method have remained.

The Wilton School occupies a state-of-the-art facility in Darien, Illinois. More than 120 courses are offered each year, including The Master Course, a 2-week class that provides individualized instruction in everything from borders to flowers to constructing a tiered wedding cake. Other courses focus on specific subjects, such as the Lambeth Method, Fondant Art and Tiered Cakes. Courses in Gum Paste and Chocolate Artistry feature personal instruction from well-known experts.

For more information or to enroll, write to:
Wilton School of Cake Decorating and Confectionery Art
2240 West 75th Street, Woodridge, IL 60517
Attn: School Coordinator

Or visit: www.school.wilton.com
Or call: 800-772-7111, ext. 2888, for a free brochure and schedule.

Wilton Method Cake Decorating Classes are the convenient way to learn to decorate, close to your home. Wilton Method Classes are easy and fun for everyone. You can learn the fundamentals of cake decorating with a Wilton-trained teacher in just four 2-hour sessions. When the course is over, you'll know how to decorate star and shell birthday cakes or floral anniversary cakes like a pro. Everyone has a good time—it's a great place for new decorators to discover their talent. Since 1974, more than 4 million people have enjoyed these courses. Special Project Classes also are available in subjects like candy-making, gingerbread, fondant, cookie blossoms and more.

Find classes near you!
In U.S.A., call 800-942-8881 or visit www.wilton.com
In Canada, call 416-679-0790, ext. 200, or email classprograms@wilton.ca
In Mexico, visit www.wiltonenespañol.com

Wilton Products

Visit a Wilton retailer near you. Your local Wilton retailer is the best place to see the great variety of cake decorating products made by Wilton. If you are new to decorating, it's a good idea to see these products in person; if you are an experienced decorator, you'll want to visit your Wilton retailer regularly to have the supplies you need on hand. From bakeware and icing supplies to candles and publications, most Wilton retailers carry a good stock of items needed for decorating. Remember, the selection of products changes with each season, so if you want to decorate cakes in time for upcoming holidays, visit often to stock up on current pans, colors and toppers.

Order on-line, by phone or by mail. You can also place orders 24 hours a day at our website, www.wilton.com. Shopping on-line is fast, easy and secure. Or, you can place an order by phone at 800-794-5866 (7WILTON) or by mail, using the Order Form in the Wilton Yearbook of Cake Decorating.

Wilton On The Web

www.wilton.com is the place to find Wilton decorating information on-line. It's filled with great decorating ideas and delicious recipes, updated regularly for the season. You'll also find helpful hints, answers to common decorating questions and easy shopping for great Wilton products.

Wilton Publications

We never run out of decorating ideas! Each year, Wilton publishes more new idea books based on Wilton Method techniques. When you're planning a specific occasion, Wilton books are a fantastic source of decorating inspiration.

The Wilton Yearbook of Cake Decorating is our annual showcase of the latest ideas in decorating. Each edition is packed with all-new cake ideas, instructions and products—it's the best place to find out what's new at Wilton. Cakes for every occasion throughout the year are included: holidays, graduations, birthdays, weddings and more. If you are looking for a new cake to test your decorating skills, you can't beat the Yearbook.

Wilton also regularly publishes special interest decorating books, including books on wedding and holiday decorating, candy-making, home entertaining and food gifting. Look for them wherever Wilton products are sold.